What people are saying about
Putting Emotional Intelligence to Work

*"This book identifies an emerging trend in corporate leadership . . .
putting emotional intelligence to work, to use Dr. Ryback's title,
means bringing out the best talents in our executives and managers,
and maybe throughout the organization."*
—ANDREAS RENSCHLER, CEO & PRESIDENT,
MERCEDES-BENZ U.S. INTERNATIONAL, INC.

*"One of the most useful and inspiring business books I have ever
read. Must reading for executives seeking to grow in interpersonal
competence. Highly and enthusiastically recommended."*
—NATHANIEL BRANDEN, PH.D., PSYCHOLOGIST, CORPORATE CONSULTANT,
AUTHOR, *The Six Pillars of Self-Esteem*

*"Terrific reading! David Ryback has discovered an exciting way to
show what's absolutely needed in business organizations."*
—MARK MAYBERRY, AUTHOR, *In the Company of Entrepreneurs*

*"David Ryback identifies what true leadership power is all about—a
refreshing, new way to manage people."*
—GREGORY P. SMITH, AUTHOR, *The New Leader*

*"This book is a must-read because it will help cut the learning curve
for managers at all levels in the organization. You might even
consider it a crash course in more effective management and
leadership."*
—CAROL A. HACKER, AUTHOR, *The High Cost of Low Morale*

*"Now, finally, David Ryback has written a book to show us how to
get in touch with our emotions and use them in a productive, professional way. People will not follow because they are TOLD or
FORCED to follow; they will follow because you are the kind of
leader they WANT to follow."*
—M. KAY DUPONT, AUTHOR, *Business Etiquette and Professionalism*

*"Fascinating! This book takes all the other management theories and
goes one step further. It contains fresh, new information that adds
significantly to our knowledge of great leadership. Most helpful."*
—JIM CAIRO, LEADERSHIP TRAINER, AUTHOR, *The Power of Effective Listening*

*"Clearly written, this book addresses the hottest topics of the day—
how motivation, performance, and productivity are all interlinked to
emotional intelligence. It is fundamental to improving relations at
all levels."*
—DR. JAMES BARRELL, PROFESSIONAL SPORTS CONSULTANT,
ORLANDO MAGIC AND SAN FRANCISCO GIANTS

Putting Emotional Intelligence to Work

Putting Emotional Intelligence to Work

Successful Leadership Is More Than IQ

David Ryback, Ph.D.

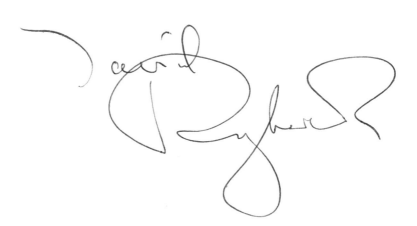

Butterworth–Heinemann
Boston   Oxford   Johannesburg   Melbourne
New Delhi   Singapore

Butterworth–Heinemann

ℛ A member of the Reed Elsevier group

Library of Congress Cataloging-in-Publication Data

Ryback, David.
    Putting emotional intelligence to work : successful leadership is more than IQ / David Ryback.
      p.   cm.
    Includes bibliographical references (p. 229) and index.
    ISBN 0–7506–9956–6 (alk. paper)
    1. Executive ability. 2. Management—Psychological aspects.
    3. Personality development. 4. Emotions and cognition. I. Title.
HD38.2.R93   1998
  658.4′09—dc21   97–15319
                                                            CIP

British Library Cataloguing-in-Publication Data
A catalogue record for this book is available from the British Library.

The publisher offers special discounts on bulk orders of this book.
For information, please contact:
Manager of Special Sales
Butterworth–Heinemann
225 Wildwood Avenue
Woburn, MA 01801-2041
Tel: 617-928-2500
Fax: 617-928-2620

For information on all Butterworth–Heinemann business books available, contact our World Wide Web home page at: http://www.bh.com

10 9 8 7 6 5

Printed in the United States of America

I don't think that I.Q. is as fungible as I used to.
To succeed, you also have to know how to make choices and
how to think more broadly.

—Bill Gates

IN MEMORIAM

In memory of Sy Ryback, the author's brother, who passed away from leukemia during the writing of this book, a portion of the royalties will be donated to the Fred Hutchinson Cancer Research Center in Seattle, Washington.

Contents

Foreword

This book identifies an emerging trend in corporate leadership—the self-managed team approach. It describes a way to more successful management at a time when rapid change has become the rule rather than the exception. We are now challenged by a global economy driven by electronic communication. The supremacy of hierarchy no longer stands. In other words, we are entering a "quantum leap" from the industrial revolution to the information revolution. Business is no longer "as usual"; as a matter of fact, it will never be the same.

Our challenge today is to restore the balance where the profit motive used to stand alone, untouched by human consideration. Of course, profit is still our main focus, but at least we can achieve such results with human dignity and social sensibility, paving the road to success with even-handed ethics and a comfortable conscience.

More than that, putting emotional intelligence to work, to use Dr. Ryback's title, means bringing out the best talents in our executives and managers and maybe throughout the entire organization. As he points out in this book, emotional intelligence is to an executive as sonar is to a ship, helping to steer clear of problem areas that can't otherwise be seen.

Why has it taken so long for business people to recognize the importance of emotional intelligence? There is no simple answer. But today's workplace demands it, if for no other reason than to deal successfully with the competition. The workplace is becoming extremely sophisticated in terms of the human counterpart to electronic communication. What executives know is just as important as what they do—emotional intelligence is clearly part of that knowledge.

Communication skills in the corporate world are more important now than ever before. And that is what emotional intelligence is all about!

—Andreas Renschler, CEO & President,
Mercedes-Benz U.S. International, Inc.

Preface

Changing Your Management Style— Forever

Steven, CEO of a successful corporation, had been very fortunate in bringing his firm to undreamed-of prosperity. Suddenly, however, he found himself isolated as his office staff, vice presidents and board all turned away from him at almost the same time, all for their own valid reasons. How could success have turned to failure in such a short time?

The qualities that allowed Steven to build the success of his firm—aggressiveness, forcefulness, boldness of intellect, intense decisiveness—were being turned inward, now that the challenge of competition with other firms had been won. Steven was still the same person, but all his forceful energies were now directed at those surrounding him rather than at the competition.

Steven himself called me in to help with what to him was a confounding dilemma. Why was everyone suddenly turning against him? He had meant to hurt no one, after all. These were supposed to be his closest allies. He could understand his conflict with the board, since he had ideas that appeared too progressive for them. But surely his VPs should back him up, he insisted.

Then a telling incident occurred. Steven and I had a difference of opinion about a scheduled meeting that he had missed. He could not recall a consult we had planned a few weeks earlier, since he had no written record if it. This might have been a very taxing difference of opinion, except for the fortunate fact that two others were part of this consult, an associate of mine and one of his. What made this incident so telling was that even with these additional witnesses, Steven continued to persevere in resisting full acceptance of what others agreed had occurred.

"It's not that I doubt your word," Steven persisted, "but I want to check my records more closely and get back to you when I've done so. I need to see a written record of this."

"Steven," I asked, "how can you doubt the words of your own associate, even if you doubt mine?"

"Well," he said, "memory can have a way of playing tricks on our minds."

I could now understand a bit better why people were turning away from Steven in droves. Although Steven wasn't calling me a liar, he certainly was making me feel like one. I felt disappointed, even though Steven was "obliging" enough to "understand" my point. I could also more fully appreciate why he'd been so successful in defeating his opponents in the marketplace. But this kind of success fails in the end, because it doesn't wear well back home. Wielding an ax may indeed conquer the foe in the field of battle, but this can also hurt those close to you if that's the only mode of communication available. I also wonder how effective such aggressive measures are in the long run, even when limited to the competition in the marketplace. Eventually, your enemies become so numerous that there's no "breathing space" left in which to survive.

I asked Steven to block any interruptions so we could talk in depth. "Do you realize," I asked him, "how you make people feel when you're so insistent on your own point of view?"

"But, David," he responded, "I only want to be sure I'm right. You know how much stress I'm under. I could easily forget such details."

"Stress?" I questioned, with as much compassion as I could muster.

"Everyone's turning against me. I've never felt so alone and vulnerable in my life. And just at a time when everything was going so successfully!"

"Do you share that vulnerability with anyone?" I asked.

"Are you out of your mind?!" he exclaimed. "Even my own lawyer has 'fired' me. How can I trust anyone?"

"Do you trust me?" was my next question.

"Well," and here Steven smiled with a slight flush in his face, "you do have your own agenda too, don't you?"

Here was a man so utterly alone that he couldn't even trust the person he had called for help.

"Steven," I finally said after a few moments of heavy silence, "if you can't trust me, then there's no point in going on."

Steven looked shocked, then embarrassed, and then this overbearing, confident, successful captain of industry broke down—not into great, heaving sobs but, just as revealing, small tears that trickled down his cheeks. For the first time in a long while, possibly in his adult life, Steven was being completely authentic. He finally let his heart come into play. And his world turned around.

A few meetings later, Steven was an ardent advocate of emotional intelligence in the workplace and allowed it to become part of his company mission.

Now Steven's firm is not only successful in the marketplace, but his board, his VPs and his office staff all think he's the greatest. Steven has taken on a leadership position in an industry-wide organization, bringing him national recognition for his communication skills on the platform. What does he speak on? Well, he doesn't call it that, but by any other name it's still . . . emotional intelligence.

If you're not yet familiar with the term, read on. In Chapter 2 you'll get an inside view of its origins. Steven learned it because he had to. Otherwise, he'd have lost everything—first his staff and then his board's support. Oh, he's still his old, competitive self, but he's become more open and authentic. Nor was he transformed overnight. As a matter of fact, he's still working on his emotional intelligence, just as I am. In this area, you never stop learning. Never.

Following my discussions with Steven, I was occasionally struck by the challenge of introducing the ideas of emotional intelligence into the workplace. Our contemporary culture seems to be struggling between two value systems—one based on achievement of dominance through political manuevering, hooliganism and social intimidation, the other based on mutual respect through emotional authenticity. From partisan politics across the Congressional aisle in Washington to such dramas as Arthur Miller's *The Crucible,* we see how personal attacks on individuals no better or worse than you or I can subject them to indefensible victimization.

In *The Crucible,* John Proctor, as hardworking and honest as any in his seventeenth-century community of Puritans, becomes subject to suspicion of witchcraft in his valiant attempt to defend his innocent wife. His only escape from hanging is to "confess" to his alliance with the Devil. In the end he chooses to hang rather than make a false confession. Amazingly, the drama ends on a high note despite his choice to die. Authenticity, in Miller's play, is a supreme value, transcending the evil machinations of an overeager and righteous agent of an otherwise benign governmental body.

This book is based on the conviction that emotional intelligence—described so well by social scientists such as E. L. Thorndike, Carl Rogers, Peter Salovey, John D. Mayer and Daniel Goleman—can play a significant role in making the workplace not only more productive and profitable, but a more meaningful and enjoyable place in which to spend a good portion of our adult lives.

In this book, you'll learn how a crisis in corporate leadership leads to a transformation in the workplace. The information age is opening up to a new value system in which mind is being joined by heart. Today's brain-driven economy cannot help but be enriched by an openness to emotional intelligence. Enhanced use of electronic technology through intranets, simulation software and push applications fall empty without human sensitivity of soul to guide the data.

Reengineering and total quality were fine but underlying all successful leadership is a quality that transcends IQ. That quality is the emotional intelligence that makes it all come together in what is ultimately a human milieu. The best laid plans of mice, humans and electronic technology can go awry without that special sensitivity.

In this book you will have the opportunity to discover the origins of emotional intelligence (going back in time over 60 years), see how it can enhance your management style, learn how to delegate and negotiate more fruitfully, how to make better use of your natural attributes and how to make your life away from work more meaningful and satisfying as well.

In Part I, I'll share with you how I first came across the concepts of emotional sensitivity while walking on the beach with a wise mentor and why feelings in information-driven workplaces are essential. In what I call the New Team Ethic, self-managed groups prove essential to success in an increasingly competitive global marketplace.

Part II presents an intimate look at the beginnings of what led to emotional intelligence as we know it today. Psychologists in the 1930s and 1940s were already writing of such concepts as "relationship process" and "social intelligence." But it wasn't until the present decade that the concept of emotional intelligence found validation in the workplace through research and Daniel Goleman's popular book, *Emotional Intelligence*. You'll read of a clear distinction between the old and new approaches, as the individual becomes more prominent in successful self-managed teams.

Part III outlines ten attributes of successful leadership and how to teach emotional intelligence to an entire organization, resulting not only in more effective management skills but in delegation and negotiation skills as well.

In Part IV, you'll learn to understand how different personalities contribute their best in an emotionally intelligent environment and how to broaden your own range of personality traits so you can become more flexible and effective. Part V concludes with some skills at home, coping with the effects of downsizing and adapting to the challenges of revolutionary changes in the modern workplace.

In addition, you'll learn the essentials necessary to bring emotions, logic and effective teamwork—the components of emotional intelligence—to successful fruition.

In order to maximize success, whether measured in dollars, morale, or in excellence, you'll examine basic assumptions, explore essentials and bring all these together for successful application of emotional intelligence in the workplace.

If you're curious about where you stand on the scale of emotional intelligence in the workplace, here's a brief survey for you to take before reading on. (A more extensive survey is in the Appendix.) Don't worry about passing or failing. This is not a standardized test—it's merely a training exercise, to help you identify the areas in which you can grow.

Ryback Emotional Quotient Executive Survey (REQuES)

Assign a number to each statement, according to the following scale:

Always	Usually	Sometimes	Rarely	Never
5	4	3	2	1

__ 1. I keep others in line so they do not overreach their assignments.

__ 2. I avoid confronting discrepancies, hoping they'll disappear in time.

__ 3. I keep my personal philosophy apart from my business personality.

___ 4. I focus on global issues, allowing others to take care of the details.
___ 5. I keep my feelings separate from any public statements.
___ 6. Intellectual "integrity" interferes with my sense of authority.
___ 7. Inner calm means more to me than spontaneous expressiveness.
___ 8. I share my personal feelings and opinions.
___ 9. I bring different factions together, even if they're opposed.
___10. I am candid with staff members about controversial findings.
___11. I make exceptions to policy to acquire important information.
___12. I give priority to the feelings leading up to a conflict.

Rather than give you the evaluation of your answers to these items now, I'll allow your emotional intelligence to unfold as you read through this book. My purpose is twofold:

1. to offer a real-time example of how an emotionally intelligent approach to education works, and
2. to motivate you to read on with a sense of curiosity that is personally relevant.

If you allow yourself an open mind, this book may change not only your style of management for the better but also the quality of your life in general. It can bring you closer to the ones who are important in your life, both at work and at home. If happiness is measured in terms of successful, meaningful relationships, then you'll be a happier person indeed. So let's begin the adventure.

Acknowledgments

After Freud and Jung brought to light the inner workings of the mind, it fell to such pioneers as Carl Rogers, Abraham Maslow and Rollo May to bring to light the importance of emotions and the relevance of authenticity—the ability to be candid and forthright in the expression of deep emotion in the moment. Of these, Rogers was the first to break with convention, back in the early 1940s, to present his case for emotionally honest communication.

I never thought I'd be writing a book dedicated to the late Carl Rogers, pioneer of radically new communication styles in psychotherapy, education, international politics and the workplace over the last half-century. When I first met this paradoxically reserved yet open-hearted man as a guest speaker in one of my graduate courses at San Diego State many moons ago, my life was substantially changed. For the first time, I heard an approach to psychology that was more real than theoretical. It opened a window to release my sensitivity from within the boundaries of my own shyness. There was now an approach, a theory, a structure of sorts that justified my reaching out to others, to bridge the gap between inner souls—mine and everyone else's.

I was instantly drawn to Rogers' ideas and, as I'll relate in Chapter 2, fate brought us together in friendship and in work. To him and to his associates in the La Jolla area, I acknowledge a debt of deep gratitude.

On a more contemporary note, I wish to thank all those who gave support and assistance in the realization of this book:

First of all, thanks go to Melitta Lewitin, who typed every word herein and edited out all the words that aren't. Her dedication and generous support will always be greatly appreciated.

To my friends and associates who read the manuscript and guided me to higher levels of written expression:

Martin C. Becker, who helped correct old memories;

Dr. Deanna Berg, who put a proper perspective on the role of honesty;

Dr. Gene Griessman, who shared his graceful sensibility whenever his input was invited;

Dr. Stephen Hamby, who asked for a survey on EQ for executives and got it;

Dr. Jaelline Jaffe, whose eye for structure will never be forgotten;

Gisela Kaufmann, Project Controller at Siemens, whose editorial suggestions raised the professional tone of the book;

Dr. Jonathan Lynton, whose candor helped maintain proper perspective;

Dr. John Powell, who shed light on the many theories of intelligence;

Dr. Steve Preston, who helped clarify the distinction between emotional and executive intelligence;

Candis Kent Stephens of Results Unlimited, whose skill with words amazed me;

Mike Stewart, always dedicated and generous with his time;

Dr. Eloise Stiglitz, who exemplifies the "listening heart" in both friendship and management style; and

C. Richard Weylman, admirable proponent of truth in management—Thank you all.

When Karen Speerstra, Publishing Director of Butterworth–

Heinemann, responded to my book proposal as music to her ears, I knew immediately that I had found the right publisher, just as I knew that I had the right editor in Stephanie Gelman Aronson when I first heard her friendly and supportive voice over the phone.

To all of you, my debt of love and gratitude continues.

1

Introduction:
Crisis in Leadership

The twentieth-century leader is somebody who tends to have
strong but hard personal qualities, somebody who is arrogant
but inspiring. However, twenty-first century leaders will be
those who can demonstrate a greater empathy and concern for
people issues and those who do not rely on position or rank for
their status.

—DR. ROBERT HAWLEY, *Engineering Management*

All of a sudden, as the new millennium begins, the concept of
emotional intelligence has begun to make its indelible mark on
the workplace. But the keen observer could see it coming for
many, many years. Successful leaders have always been attuned
to human interaction and their decisions were imbued with emotional sensitivity. But this was hardly ever discussed openly;
rather it was like an underground secret. Finally, the underlying
essence of successful leadership is being revealed for all to
consider.

The concept of emotional intelligence was born at the beginning of the decade. In 1990, Peter Salovey and John D. Mayer

1

published the first paper on this topic. Even decades before that, though, the renowned psychologist E. L. Thorndike (1935) wrote of social intelligence—the capacity to "act wisely in human relations." But the popularity of the notion didn't take off until Daniel Goleman's best-selling book, *Emotional Intelligence*, was published in 1995.

LEADERSHIP: STATE OF THE ART

There is a crisis in corporate leadership today—ask any top executive. The industrial revolution was always focused on productivity and achievement with little concern for human sensibilities. But as we are taken by storm at the advent of accelerating dependence on electronic communication in the information revolution, the human brain is receiving more respect than ever. Yet intellectual capital is a concept that is troubling to many.

For one thing, it's becoming clear that although mind can be separated from heart, the two are intertwined at some level if human integrity is to be maintained. Otherwise, we have robot-like decisions, and computers can do that by themselves very well, thank you. It's apparent that what we need is a finely tuned combination of mind and heart.

The corporate landscape has shifted dramatically as we enter the twenty-first century, becoming both intensely competitive as well as mutually interactive at the same time, as paradoxical as that may seem.

Corporate leadership styles have been a focus of attention as never before, with particular focus on development of leadership skills at top levels of management as they make this influence felt throughout the organization.

COMPETITION ACROSS THE ELECTRONIC GLOBE

The most apparent shift in the corporate landscape is the advent of electronic communication, fulfilling Marshall McLuhan's prophecy of a global village. Geopolitical boundaries are increasingly ignored as communication on the Internet spans the globe in milliseconds. Market boundaries become blurred: they used to consist of lines on a map; now they're demographic statistics. Regulatory shifts become increasingly difficult to follow and keep up with.

With such dynamic forces coming into play at an accelerating rate, competition for market shares has become intense, not only domestically but globally as well.

The product itself, with a greatly shortened life cycle, has given way to customer service as the added value that differentiates winner from loser.

So how can the successful corporation succeed in this increasingly competitive marketplace? Well, since the customer remains as strongly influenced as ever by cost of the product at the point of sale, reduction of unit cost is still important. Beyond that, corporate leaders have to respond with shorter production cycles and greater flexibility all around in terms of management style through the ranks.

Over the years, we've seen sincere efforts at transforming management to respond to the challenge, from Quality Circles to reengineering, from downsizing to outsourcing, all of which failed to change the fundamental approach of most companies.

HIRING AND HOLDING

The internal dynamics of corporate leadership have changed drastically as well. There has been a shift in many organizations away from hierarchy to decentralization. Emphasis on job security has given way to skill diversity. The executive suite has given way to the virtual office, where Internet technology allows for the flexibility needed by the globally mobile executive. Issues of succession are giving way to choices for top positions made on the basis of specific skills and the flexibility to adapt quickly to new challenges.

Job security? Forget it! Newly graduated MBAs' cynical responses to this dilemma is to move around their first few years instead of choosing one company to build a career with. They pick up some skills, then move on to acquire some newer skills; this results in a mercenary attitude unheard of until now. I've heard one recent graduate say, "I'll be there, make my mark and move on."

Job descriptions at the top are becoming obsolete. Employment security is becoming an oxymoron. New forms of assessment are on the rise in an attempt to capture what executive skills work best. Academic debates at future forums allow corporations to share their challenges and tentative solutions with one another. Training curricula are moving targets, evading the essentials that can be nailed down because we're so preoccupied trying to keep up with the business of business. Collective concepts such as "creative leadership" and "talent alliance" only further substantiate the fact that we're painfully plodding along, weighed down by the fear that the best executives feel more like part of a temporary agency than an elite corps of leaders.

It's not uncommon for rising young executives to spend six months in one department before being transferred to another department to develop their repertoire—much unlike the one- or two-year stints of prior years. Many volunteer for special assignments to advance their own portfolio.

All this just points out more clearly the need to understand the crisis in leadership and how to make it work under these trying circumstances. Given the challenges inherent in restructuring and downsizing, how does an organization hold on to the best and the brightest? Career paths no longer assure loyalty to a single company. The information revolution means skill flexibility and the resulting mobility if it means anything at all to management. To the individual executive, it means adopting an emotionally intelligent attitude to improve one's own situation as well as that of the organization.

Successful executives are being tempted by more external offers than ever before. Consequently, the nature of employment contracts are changing as well. More sophisticated leveraged and restricted stock options packages have replaced company loyalty as the guiding factor for holding on to successful executives; successful, young executives are highly marketable and are willing to pick up and go if the price is right.

This opportunistic ethic has created a much more dynamic orientation in the corporate world. One effective response to the consequent potential of instability has been to turn to the replacement strategy of team focus.

360-DEGREE ASSESSMENT

This means open communication and leadership, which is much more responsive to "360-degree" assessment with multiple data from multisource feedback. Any staff member having worked in the past with the executive being assessed may be requested to fill out a rating form to assess that executive. An outside consultant typically takes on the task of feeding back this pooled information to the executive.

This has the advantage of consensus, as opposed to a single individual's view, which might be contaminated by personal prejudice. Consensus can also be obtained in real-time "team feedback" in which working teams discuss their own shortcomings in open forum, including the possibility of exploring the pros and cons of their own leader's style in that individual's presence. Although this takes a high degree of trust among the team members, the result can be highly effective in enhancing team "bonding."

In an earlier era, providing such feedback to the "boss" would have been unheard of, especially by the "boss" himself. Today, there is more likely to be a democratically-oriented team leader who shares the focus of responsibility among the team members rather than among a closely held cadre of personal favorites.

ENDS AND MEANS

The greatest challenge to understanding today's crisis in leadership is to break it down to its basic components. In order to do so, the category of bottom-line results has been complemented by that of competencies or behaviors. In other words, in addition to bottom-line dollar figures, we are also looking at the means used to achieve the results.

In the past, a top executive's performance was measured primarily by such bottom-line measures as financial return on capital, assets or equity or such internal processes as unit cost, cycle time, asset utilization or speed to market. Now there is a greater tendency to include customer reactions such as satisfaction, brand image, segment performance and market share as well as internal factors such as employee satisfaction, turnover and diversity.

Successful leadership now includes guidance and empowering ability along with productivity and achievement. The successful leader is now seen more as a motivator of purpose and alignment and an inspiration to corporate commitment. There is a greater need to optimize for ongoing change over the long term. The Japanese concept of continual improvement has spilled over to influence American executives to continue learning and finding creative ways of dealing with new challenges. Changes are so rapid now that there is a desperate need to recognize emerging patterns to make the necessary connections to successful outcome. Being a visionary is no longer sufficient; that must be followed up with successful alignment and implementation.

THE SEVEN CORE QUALITIES OF LEADERSHIP

A number of corporations have made attempts at defining the core competencies of successful leadership, and each of these has its own subculture of language to struggle with these issues. After looking at a number of corporate measures of successful leadership, I've attempted to identify the core qualities that run through all of them. In Figure 1-1, I've isolated seven core qualities that, in my estimation, run throughout the lists of leadership qualities as determined by AT&T, Chevron, Citicorp, General Electric, Honeywell and Pepsi-Co.

	AT&T	Chevron	Citicorp	G.E.	Honeywell	Pepsi
Strategic Planning	Planning proactively	Strategy development	Leadership	Initiative/ speed	Strategic thinking	Thinking outside the box
Communication & Alignment	Clarity	Communication alignment	Proficiency	Communication/ influence	Communication	Alignment
Team Building	Team effectiveness	Teamwork & partnership	Relationship	Team builder	Teamwork & cooperation	Team leadership
Continuous Learning	Openness to learning	Learning organization	Execution skills	Knowledge/ expertise	Personal mastery	Intellectual curiosity
Dynamic Accountability	Accountability	Trust & achievement	Professional standards	Accountability/ commitment	High professional standards	Professional maturity
Systemic Results	Implements with excellence	Measurement & achievement	Operating results	Influence	Execution	Organizational impact
Actualized Integrity	Self-awareness	Honesty & integrity	Social responsibility	Integrity	Vision & values	Integrity

Figure 1-1. Core Values in Successful Leadership

1. Strategic Planning

Strategic planning is a holdover from the last wave of popular management training programs, an artifact originally used to clarify missions for mid-level managers and below. It retains its former quality of immediate problem solving but now replaces what used to be called "comprehensive planning," employed at division level and above.

2. Communication and Alignment

The New Team Ethic (see Chapter 5) is clearly influential here. Alignment used to mean hierarchical communication from an autocratic source, but now it implies that the organization supports individual empowerment, a sense of egalitarian inclusion and a team approach. Alignment used to involve merely five, six or seven individuals with hierarchical levels of responsibility. Now it tends to involve the identification of an array of characteristics necessary to successfully achieve a mission, involving a larger number of people working closely together.

3. Team Building

Simple hierarchy as a leadership style is dead. Period. Teams embedded in a modified hierarchy are the trend.

4. Continuous Learning

In the past, learning was assumed to be complete by the time an individual graduated from college. Now, the learning process is highly valued and practiced throughout the modern organization, with internal "universities" and a commitment to continuing education. AT&T refers to this as "openness to learning" and Pepsi as "intellectual curiosity."

5. Dynamic Accountability

Simple accountability in the past referred primarily to bottom-line, profit-based figures. Today it gives equal weight to the means used to accomplish the ends as well. Terms such as "professional standards" used by Citicorp and Honeywell and "professional maturity" used by Pepsi exemplify this change.

6. Systemic Results

As in accountability, results in the past were derived from unidimensional sources. Today, results are gleaned from all facets and levels of the organizational operation. We learned, slowly, from the Japanese that attending to multiple factors could be profitable.

7. Actualized Integrity

In former lists of organizational priorities, integrity, if not altogether ignored, was deemed a disposable luxury. Today, emphasis on customer satisfaction as added value forces companies to be more mindful of issues of integrity. Increased consumer awareness makes unwavering integrity a market plus. Note Honeywell's priority of "vision and values" and Citicorp's "social responsibility."

Clearly, there is more to successful leadership than mere IQ. Team-building and integrity, for example, have more to do with heart than brain. Values are just as important as strategy. Every company needs a central leadership strategy, which takes all this into account.

Whatever approach is employed, it is essential that the CEO express a commitment to the time and energy necessary to initiate, complete and follow up on the program if the initiative comes from a VP. Such commitment (or lack of it) will filter down the line ultimately to affect the program as a whole. The biggest mistake is to initiate and employ a program of leadership development without the total commitment of the top officer.

MILITARY EMOTIONAL INTELLIGENCE

Even the military has seen its management style transform over time. Historically, when battles were led by individual commanders such as Caesar and Napoleon, the directing style was most appropriate. Blind obedience to authority was the rule. By the Civil War and certainly by World Wars I and II, gigantic armies driven by more efficient firepower and technology were forcing a more participatory form of leadership in which commanders consulted increasingly with their generals. In the modern military, top leaders are forced to delegate more and more responsibility to subordinates, since success in combat is now more a matter of virtually instantaneous reaction to technological challenges.

Between 1862 and 1864, Abraham Lincoln was frustrated with the outcome of battles raging between the North and South. Despite the fact that he chose his generals on the basis of their having few weaknesses, the South was successfully overcoming the Union's superiority in manpower and matériel.

Lincoln's problem was in choosing his generals on the basis of overall qualifications while his southern counterpart, Robert E. Lee, was choosing his generals on the basis of their single, unique strengths as they applied to their particular missions. Stonewall Jackson and other Confederate generals had some great personal weaknesses, but unique personal strengths.

Lee's emotionally intelligent choice of generals, on the basis of strengths matched to particular missions, almost made up for the Union's superiority in men and matériel. Only when Lincoln finally appointed General Ulysses S. Grant did the tide turn in his favor.

KEEPING THE PERSONAL SEPARATE FROM BUSINESS

Paradoxically, emotionally intelligent executives, though warm, open and communicative, must keep their friendships separate from the decision-making process on personnel. Since it is important that the right person be selected for a particular job, favoritism or personal preference cannot interfere.

This means that the emotionally intelligent leader maintains a consistent level of warmth and openness to all staff members without preference based on personal similarities or history of friendship. The old style of leadership, in many cases, meant a consistently cold and aloof attitude to all, with occasional exceptions based on private considerations. The emotionally intelligent approach treats all with sincere warmth on a consistent basis. This is possible because of the support the leader experiences from below in the ongoing flow of honest, supportive feedback.

Close personal relationships can still be enjoyed, but cannot be the basis of work-related communication. Emotionally intelligent leaders transcend their personal needs at the workplace. They have the flexibility to let appropriate attitudes rise to particular occasions, a trait that is characteristic of emotionally intelligent leadership. What is of paramount importance is that the right person fit any particular job, independent of other personal proclivities.

APPRECIATING PERSONAL STRENGTHS

In order for executives to make emotionally intelligent decisions, they must have a genuine liking for people in general along with unusually high self-esteem. A strong self-image allows for greater independence in making decisions that others may find unfavorable. Some may even consider the best executives as somewhat cavalier, and that may be the way things ought to be. As long as that leader is consistently warm and open to others while still objective and fair in making decisions, a great sense of self-admiration may not necessarily be bad.

In the twenty-first century, the criteria for leadership will be not only knowledge and experience, but also healthy self-esteem and sensitivity to others' feelings. A successful organization will have a person with a high degree of all four factors at the helm.

Executives' most important decisions are those promoting the personal growth of their staff members in such a way that they will contribute to a successful enterprise. Each individual's strongest features will be applied in the areas where they can best be used. As a result each individual can feel fully appreciated for what is offered to the corporate mission.

Feeling fully appreciated, such individuals can turn around and reciprocate their leader's good will by doing all in their power to support their leader in critical times, even when human frailty becomes evident (as happens occasionally to all, even emotionally intelligent CEOs).

The key to effective support is seeing the cup as half full, looking for the strengths of individuals rather than their weaknesses, and building on those strengths. The key to making emotionally intelligent decisions is to focus on the end result of each person's contribution, from entry-level worker to top executive.

Emotionally intelligent management decisions are also forward-looking, focusing on opportunities rather than problems, forging new directions into the next century instead of fortifying old ones, and identifying new levels of excellence.

THE ART OF COMPROMISE

Some decisions an executive must face relate to the balance between morality and pragmatism—weighing what is philosophically and politically correct versus what is the most profitable approach. Under the New Team Ethic, this approach takes into consideration the free-flowing input from VPs and their team leaders, although such decisions are ultimately the sole responsibility of the CEO. Here's where being in touch with one's emotions is extremely helpful.

Once the decision is made, the executive can communicate directly with the staff members most directly involved with the implementation of the decision to ensure it meets with the understanding and expectations of the executive who must ultimately take full responsibility.

Emotionally intelligent decision making involves, first and foremost, a consideration of whether a given decision falls into the category of policy—where it has a history of similar decisions made in the past—or is an exception and therefore requires attention to underlying assumptions and values, necessary when new conditions are taken into consideration.

If the decision falls into the "exception" category, then full attention must be paid to the ethical values surrounding the issue before implementation strategies are considered. Since implementation always involves some degree of compromise, it is much easier to consider the ethics affected *independent* of implementation. Then, after implementation has been carried out, there will be a clearer corporate conscience through which to examine the results.

This type of thinking helps in appreciating long-term trends and their effect on company goals. This emotionally intelligent approach to decision making provides for a more consistent corporate philosophy, as well as a more reliable path to ongoing profits with fewer costly mistakes.

Sometimes what seems like a minor point can be a major problem in disguise, and this will only be revealed when the important value surfaces at a later time. An emotionally intelligent executive can resist the temptation of yielding to momentary pressures in order to consider deeper values early on when that is necessary.

TAKING RESPONSIBILITY

The overriding unique quality of a successful executive is the unreserved acceptance of full responsibility for any decision made under present leadership. All others on the team have the benefit of the doubt. Like the one rifleman shooting a blank among the squad of executioners, each can avoid assumption of responsibility for a bad decision—but not the responsible executive. That individual alone stands responsible, despite the process of self-management by consensus and the free flow of opinion. A compromise is bound to come up against some resistance, if not by both sides, then at least by one.

In order to survive this burden with the fewest misgivings, the emotionally intelligent executive can become familiar with the details relating to difficult decisions first-hand, not through second-hand reports. This means actually going to the site where the decision will be implemented and interacting directly with those most directly involved.

By the time a difficult decision reaches the responsible executive, it is bound to be complicated. Otherwise, it would have been resolved before reaching their desk. Dealing with the most difficult decisions, this individual is best armed with common sense, direct experience and qualitative parameters. These can best be obtained by:

- A free flow of information from all involved parties.
- Organized information in the form of relevant data.
- The executive's physical presence and direct interaction at the point of implementation—from time to time during normal operations, but immediately at any crisis.

The emotionally intelligent leader needs all the information that can be gleaned from every source in order to make the best high-level decisions. A leader who missteps may not be around very long—such is the burden of leadership!

FROM "NEW" LEMONS TO "CLASSIC" LEMONADE: A CASE OF EMOTIONALLY INTELLIGENT MANAGEMENT

"A new type of leader is required," according to British CEO, Robert Hawley, "one who understands the value of information technology, one who can satisfy customer and shareholder expectations, and the greater aspirations of employees" (1996, p. 217). In the history of management, points out Hawley, we've gone from single-minded dictatorship wherein the market and competition were limited by regional or national borders to today's leaders who are multiskilled and multidisciplinary team leaders dealing with an international marketplace. As the future unfolds, he concludes, "we are rediscovering 'people' values."

The bigger the corporation, the greater the need for executive intelligence to help solve problems, usually involving breakdowns in communication, and this can be very time intensive. Each such incident seems to be unique. The emotionally intelligent executive can cut through much of this time by searching for the feeling behind the problem, the subtext underlying the context. That's where the essential conflict can be most easily exposed. This is one area where the executive's intuitive abilities can be very practical. The emotionally intelligent executive can cut to the heart of the matter. For a contemporary example, let's take a look at a very familiar and successful organization.

After almost 100 years of successfully selling the exact same product, Coca-Cola decided to mix things up. Since its inception in 1886, the top-secret Merchandise 7 formula for Coke had never been changed, except for removing a minute amount of cocaine in 1903. But in 1985, a secret marketing test of 190,000 consumers revealed to Coke's management that a lighter, sweeter New Coke would compete more successfully with Pepsi.

We all know what happened after that. Coke had made what can arguably be described as the worst marketing decision since Ford's Edsel. Of course, Coke was able to regroup and turn the apparent fiasco into what some now argue was the most brilliant marketing ploy—turning the media attention into free publicity as it brought back its original product, now called Classic Coke. The combination of New Coke and Classic Coke was a resounding victory over Coke's closest rival, Pepsi.

However things turned out, the inaccuracy of the consumer test lay in a lack of emotional intelligence in this particular project for an otherwise successful company. The consumer test was well run but lacked sufficient depth in its emotional component. The American consumer had a special connection to Coke and the test failed to tap this deep attachment. Even if New Coke did better on taste tests, the divorce from the original would not be without emotional consequence.

It was like the death of a father, according to Coca-Cola Chairman Roberto Goizueta. "You know you're going to be sad," he said. "You're never going to know how sad you'll be—the depth of your sorrow—until he's dead." If the test marketing had been more emotionally intelligent, peering into the consumers' feelings as well as their taste buds, this gargantuan mistake could have been avoided.

Coke loyalists were up in arms at this marketing decision. Goizueta and his associates had to admit their mistake in the glare of public censure. But, quick on his feet, Goizueta was able to turn lemons into lemonade by renaming the old standby Coca-Cola Classic and making it available alongside its new sibling, New Coke.

As an emotionally intelligent executive, Roberto Goizueta was quick to respond to the glitch in the curve. His reaction was not only responsible, it was (equally important) responsive. Instead of getting into a defensive mode, he accepted the new reality and embedded it into Coca-Cola's continuous success curve.

Much of Goizueta's success was due to his ability to communicate with both his staff, who were caught up in this marketing fiasco, and also with the public, through the media. Lesser executives might have divorced themselves from the problem area and shunned the media during such a crisis, but not Goizueta, adept at understanding others' reactions and communicating with that knowledge in mind.

Moral of the story? It is essential to integrate all the departments in a concerted team effort at accomplishing the best possible outcome. Since the New Coke incident, Coca-Cola has invested a lot of effort in becoming more pro-active, making Coca-Cola one of the ten best-performing companies in recent years. Its novel marketing ideas (a dimpled Sprite bottle, a plastic contour bottle and the introduction of two new competitive soft drinks) make it even more successful in terms of revenue, net income and happier shareholders.

But all this takes a team effort, from chemists to product development to finance. Reports CEO Goizueta (according to news articles by Chris Roush), "We expect every employee to think creatively. I realize that the marketing side or the product side is the one people see most. [But] some of these come from engineering. Others come from marketing. Others come from suggestions from our associates. It's not just new products or packaging" (1997, p. E4).

What are the specific qualities that contribute to the emotional intelligence of this eminently successful leader? First of all, according to Roush, Goizueta enjoys his role as a leader and offers a model for effective leadership. Although modest and soft-spoken, he nonetheless "thoroughly enjoys being in charge ... he's having a good time," according to Frederick Allen, author of Coca-Cola's history *The Secret Formula* (Roush, 1996, p. H3).

Goizueta is able to take responsibility for any problem and convert apparent mistakes to advantage. He got directly involved, faced the reality of the facts as they were and, with hardly a glitch, resolved into a marketing miracle what could have been a disaster under less emotionally intelligent leadership. It even left some marketing mavens wondering whether the whole fiasco was engineered on purpose. Goizueta approached the problem boldly and created success out of apparent failure.

Goizueta has the ability to bring out the best in others, helping them to grow and develop themselves. He grooms his executives by moving them around to furnish them with the experience he feels they need. His genuinely felt concern for others results in a deep sense of loyalty from his staff members. He fosters a sense of genuine honesty by encouraging his staff members to be totally open with him. "I used to fight with him all the time," says former Chief Financial Officer Sam Ayoub. "The beauty about him is I could go and close the door with him and tell him I disagreed with him. He doesn't like cowards" (Roush, 1996, p. H3).

Goizueta is particularly sensitive to matching his staff members to projects for which they're best suited. "The chief executive has ultimate responsibility to decide what to delegate and to whom," he maintains. "If you pick the right person, you'll come out smelling like a rose" (Roush, 1996, p. H3).

CONCLUSION

Emotionally intelligent executives are bottom-line people who can deal with glitches by keeping their eyes on the ultimate goal, by controlling the impulse to give in to momentary crises and by focusing on the long term. They put effort into understanding the viewpoints of superiors as well as staff members and communicate appropriately with that in mind. They use their emotions to fine-tune their intuition as they steer the company in the right direction above the fray of complex details. They are open to dissenting opinions and can find their overall direction because they trust their own feelings.

The emotionally intelligent executive is incisive in choosing leadership qualities, and is adept at keeping personal prejudices from interfering with the appreciation of others' strengths in the domain of interpersonal sensitivity, thereby promoting a strong sense of loyalty. Balancing pragmatism with morality, he considers exceptions to policy when deeper values merit such decisions, exploring the matter with a physical presence on site, organized information in the form of hard copy and an ear to consensus.

So where does the process of emotional intelligence come from? Where did it originate? Well, let me tell you a story—my story—about conversations that took place while walking along the beach.

Part I
Why Feelings in the Workplace?
(Because They're There!)

"Let's focus on a particular type of relationship to test our thinking. What about boss and employee?"

"Sounds good," I say. "How could we remove the power dynamic . . . and would it still work?"

"Well, we'd have to start with the boss, since he's the one with the power," says Carl. "What would he be like if he were authentic instead of 'bossy' in the negative sense—manipulative and without heart? Let's examine how these two individuals would be different if we 'humanized' them."

"First of all, I guess, we'd have to create a feeling of safety, so they'd feel free to experiment with opening up."

"Well, that would be the responsibility of the boss, since he's clearly in charge," says Carl. "He'd have to at least be a com-passionate type, easy to talk to and have the desire to help rather than just 'boss' his employees."

"More than that," I add, "he'd have to be able to take satisfaction in the growth of his employees, and not be threatened by it."

"Yes," agrees Carl, "he'd have to be willing to give up his power, at least the artificial part that comes from his being put in that position rather than by earning it, and be able to find it more meaningful to extend himself and give away as much of the artificial part of the power as possible."

"What about unconditional positive regard," I ask, "doing away with any sense of judgment? How does that part of your theory fit in?"

"Well, that's certainly essential."

"Especially if the employee were lazy," I add.

"Actually," says Carl, "I think if the employee were treated more as an equal, he'd probably act more responsibly. Laziness can be a reaction to . . ."

"Bossiness?"

"Yes," Carl smiles, "if someone feels like he's being regulated. And with less regulation, you probably wouldn't need as many bosses. A lot of 'bossing' has more to do with 'regulating' than leading toward success."

"So in your system, there'd be more equality, more sharing of power, more . . ."

"I know there'd be more caring," says Carl, "more real caring about the employee's success and welfare. And the boss would be more likely to get his feet wet and do his part, rather than just order others to get the job done."

2

A Walk on the Beach

The real act of discovery consists not in finding new lands but in seeing with new eyes.

—MARCEL PROUST

Imagine an office of upbeat individuals practically anticipating each other's needs. Communication is buzzing—there are few misunderstandings, no blaming. The flow is productive and seamless. Impossible, you say? This is the norm when leaders use the New Team Ethic. The time has finally come.

The corporation that allows for compassion, mutual support and candor in all matters relevant to success of the organization will outperform all others. Sure, it's important to be tough in the business world. People rarely get ahead in business by being weak. But compassion, support and candor do not come from weakness. They come from courage—the ability to put yourself on the line, to make a tough judgment call and have the guts to stick to it, even when the going gets rough. They come from searching your heart for the right word and the tenacity of keeping that word, even though you may feel completely alone when first uttering it. Emotional intelligence is far from weakness. It derives from inner strength which, when joined to a sensitive heart, makes for real character.

Putting emotional intelligence to work is more than a flight of fantasy for corporate America. It's the most effective way to get more productive results in today's extremely competitive marketplace.

Before an executive can unleash the potential of staff members for great contribution, there must be a supportive community in which all are motivated to speak from the heart, with personal integrity. Herein lies the essence of emotional intelligence in the workplace: Honesty within promotes honesty on the outside. Blocks to success will be more quickly identified. Creative, breakthrough thinking will be more frequent; and difficult answers will come down on the side of integrity and success, avoiding ethical and costly legal problems.

Such success, however, does not come without a price—it requires courage, dedication, honesty and commitment, even in the face of intense differences of opinion:

- Courage to persist with ideas that are not yet proven, which may precipitate the challenge of resistance
- Dedication to hear each voice as a potential breakthrough regardless of how softly it comes across
- Honesty to be forthcoming with your deepest convictions even if they fly in the face of the day's popular banner
- Commitment to your ideals and to the process, accepting the pain that is often essential to becoming effective at the deepest levels

The overriding value in all this is *relevance*, both to the organization's success as well as to the integrity of each individual. As long as an individual comes from a place of authenticity, then that person deserves the respect of the group. Ultimately, the best team takes to heart the sensibilities of all its members. With a greater sense of trustworthiness, a team, a committee, a board, a CEO will be more successful than its less-trusting counter-part. Emotional intelligence is one path that can lead to such success.

The three greatest challenges in the workplace are, always have been, and always will be, organization, motivation and conflict resolution. Intellect can do much to resolve such challenges, but omitting the heart's input is akin to fighting with one hand tied. The more competition in the workplace the greater the risk of leaving out the heart—emotional intelligence.

Imagine you're the coach of a football team, an underdog playing against a superior team, down by 6 points at half-time, and it's do or die for a play-off berth. You've got less than 10 minutes at half-time to turn things around. You know your team has the raw material—you've just got to push them to release their potential. Consider two scenarios—one in which you use logic and reason alone, the other in which you use mind and heart. Of course, heart will win out virtually every time! Does this metaphor speak to the workplace? I think so!

THE BASIS OF EMOTIONAL INTELLIGENCE

I remember when I first became aware of the elements making up emotional intelligence. The warm sun glittered playfully on the shimmering ocean waves as I walked along the beach with Carl Rogers, eminent psychologist and pioneering founder of client-centered therapy. That was at least 15 years ago.

The story begins even earlier than that. At the time I was a fledgling assistant professor at a small, rural Georgia college. Having arrived fairly recently from the diverse and sophisticated city of Montreal, my hometown, I felt very much like a fish out of water in this conservative, rural milieu. The chairman of my department probably saw me as a nuisance who most likely wouldn't last more than a year or two.

One day the department phone rang. "Can I speak to Dr. Ryback?"

"He's not in his office right now," answered my chairman. "Who should I say called?"

"Could you have him call me back?" asked the midwestern voice. "This is Carl Rogers."

Can you imagine the expression on the face of my colleague, doctoral degree and all notwithstanding! I wasn't there, but from the way he told others about it later, I'm sure his jaw dropped at least a few inches. Whether he said it or not, I have no idea, but I'm sure he at least thought to himself, "*The* Carl Rogers?"

At the time Rogers was, except for B. F. Skinner, the best-known living psychologist. He was well known by students of psychology worldwide for his innovations in counseling and psychotherapy. Client-centered therapy involves careful non-judgmental listening and conveying back to the client that she is clearly appreciated and, more than that, prized for who she is, regardless of what hidden skeletons rattled out of the proverbial closet. By mirroring clients' deepest, unspoken emotions, Rogers found that they grew in confidence and self-esteem and began to choose options that proved productive not only for them but for those around them as well. Carl Rogers was the first to teach the enhancing skills of empowerment. In his later years, Rogers explored the application of those skills in education and eventually in the arena of international politics.

That's when I got to know Carl Rogers.

When I first arrived in Georgia, I founded a national conference on education. When I suggested we invite Carl Rogers to be our keynote speaker, the planning committee had a good laugh. "Are you joshin'?" they asked collectively. "Carl Rogers—come to our little college? Let's get serious!"

Too naive to be discouraged, I called information for Rogers' number in La Jolla, California, and simply invited him to come. "I don't do conferences any more," he replied, "but tell me about your program anyway."

I told him about the innovations to education with which some of us at the college were experimenting, and he was sufficiently impressed to say, "I think I have something to learn from what you're doing. I'll accept your invitation."

So Carl Rogers and I became friends, quickly warming to one another as soon as I picked him up one balmy summer afternoon at the Atlanta airport. The conference was eminently successful, thanks in no small part to Rogers' participation, and he and I continued to correspond from time to time, and I occasionally visited him in La Jolla.

Rogers had the habit of taking a daily stroll on the beach near his very comfortable home in the La Jolla hills every afternoon. He invited me to join him and I was quite pleased to do so. We'd take the short drive down to the beach, doff our shoes and walk barefoot along the surf, discussing whatever crossed our minds.

I wish I could recall the exact words of some of those talks. The best I can do is capture the mood and essence of some of our more germane discussions and put words to those memories. To recapture the mood, and whatever recollections I can, it helps to visualize the beautiful surf Carl and I walked along, step by barefoot step, allowing the waves to lap at our ankles and occasionally stopping to watch some seagulls soar on the horizon or notice in appreciation as a father and young son passed a ball back and forth . . .

"Having tested the waters of education and international politics, Carl, what's next? Does the business world interest you at all?"

"I haven't yet had the opportunity to do so but, yes, it would be nice to know if businesspeople could become gentler and less competitive in their endeavors. What makes you ask?"

"Well, the business world has always interested me. We tend to think of business in terms of power dynamics. I wonder . . . if people could become more honest, maybe even supportive in general, would that make them less successful?" I flash a broad grin. "Or more?"

Carl glances at me and the grin catches on. "Hmm . . . ," he smiles with interest, "what a provocative thought! Tell me more."

"Well, if people can be better therapists and teachers by being authentic and supportive, and that even works in the arena of politics, why not in business?"

"Because business is often manipulative," he returns, "although I wish it weren't so."

"Any more so than politics?" I parry.

"Well, you've got a point there. Maybe I'm judging too quickly. So . . . what would happen if business people were more authentic?"

"That's what I meant to ask you, Carl."

"Okay, let's think it through together."

And so the two of us enter into a dialog about the dynamics of leadership and power in the work setting, and how to attain the most effective form of management. We talk about the place of authenticity and compassion and the comparative merits of regulation versus equality, of manipulation versus candor. Eventually, we come to Rogers' version of effective communication between boss and employee.

1. LESS HIERARCHY, MORE LOYALTY

"So at each step of the way," I say, "the employee needs, or at least could use, honest feedback—less hierarchy and more understanding feedback."

"You see," now Carl is beginning to show signs of excitement, "that's where the magic comes in—that special feeling when two people are really communicating, when the formality is given up and a real sharing takes place, so both people are learning."

"What's the boss learning?" I ask, knowing the answer, but wanting to hear it in Carl's own words.

"The magic of careful attentiveness to someone whose welfare you care about," he says with that special glint in his eye, articulating the elegant simplicity of his theory better than an armful of textbooks. "If that employee really feels listened to and understood—deeply understood—then he will work to the best of his ability, be eager to grow and will feel intensely loyal to his company."

2. LEADERSHIP BY PARTNERING

"Yes, I've seen the data," I say. "When people feel deeply understood, they feel more secure."

"Not only deeply understood," adds Carl, "but also with emotional honesty and a sense of . . . fragility, or frailty or. . . ." He twirls his forefinger, searching for the right word.

"Vulnerability?" I ask.

"Yes, that's it! A sense of vulnerability so that the employee doesn't feel all alone in risk-taking and making mistakes. The boss needs to be authentic so all feelings, strong or weak, can be expressed. Only that way can there be a true partnership in the risk-taking."

3. THE POWER OF DEEP LISTENING

"You know, it's interesting, Carl, that both you and I have fairly reserved personalities, and here we are talking about expressing emotions. I could blame my Canadian background. You could blame your midwestern upbringing. Does that make it harder for us to express our feelings?"

"Well, I can just speak for myself," he answers. "I was very shy as a child and maybe I still am, but . . . that doesn't stop me from being honest about my feelings in words. I don't have to jump up and down to say I'm happy or sob out loud to say I'm sad. No, that's no excuse. One can still be emotionally honest without a great display of emotion. What's your feeling about this, David?"

I'm caught off guard for the moment as we walk on in silence, giving me a chance to think. He remains patient, allowing me freedom of reflection.

"I've thought about that a lot, Carl. I sometimes admire people who are easily expressive. I find I'm often misunderstood because I'm sometimes not as spontaneous about my feelings as I'd like to be."

"Kind of apart from others?" he asks, "as if they don't like you . . . or respect or appreciate you?"

Darn if I don't feel a jab of something or other cutting through me—not a bad feeling—more like a mild jolt of electricity. I've already come to recognize this as something that occasionally happens when Carl cuts through my defenses with his simple, yet incisive, questions. Here is the essential Rogerian process, in the flesh, so to speak—caring, deep attention that cuts right through conventional talk, a uniquely different form of communication for which there is no name, other than that of Rogers. I'm flushed with emotion. All I can come up with is, "Yes, I guess that's true."

Carl doesn't pursue any further emotional response from me, totally comfortable with the ensuing silence, and I feel enlarged by that somehow. No need to explain, or defend or open myself any further. That is the unique quality of the man, Carl Rogers. I feel strangely in the presence of the pure essence of integrity, and I must attribute it to him since I feel this special feeling no place else. Now I understand more fully why so many people from such diverse walks of life have such love and reverence for this shy, homespun man.

4. "SELLING" TRUST

I search for a segue that will bring us back to the topic of business.

> "If only we could bottle that level of trust that enables people to work together so effectively, and sell it," I say playfully. Then, more seriously, "There must be a way to train leaders for that kind of trust, to teach people how to be open and persist through the initial awkwardness and confusion."
>
> "Yes, I agree," says Carl. "My experience in groups is that there is almost always some awkwardness and confusion at first. As a matter of fact, I would even go so far as to say that a group never really gels until the leader deals honestly with it. It really remains superficial until that initial confusion—about less structured leadership and organization—has been dealt with."
>
> "So how would you teach that?" I ask.
>
> "All I can do is be myself in any group," he replies, "my total, honest self. If people can trust me, my honesty and openness, my frankness, then maybe they'll take a risk on being open themselves."
>
> "I've certainly seen that happen around you," I say. "Groups seem to blossom and flower when you're a part of them. I've never seen that anywhere else."

"You're very kind," he says, "but all I can do is be myself. If that encourages others, so much the better."

"I marvel at how you do that, Carl. It seems so unique, so different. Certainly, other members of the group aren't lying. They're being honest too, presumably, so why is your honesty so much more... powerful... so potent in encouraging others to lower their guard, take down their defenses?"

Carl is silent for a moment. "I don't exactly know," he says finally. "All I can say is I share my feelings as honestly and straight-forwardly as I can, particularly those that persist in me for a while."

"Would it be accurate to say that you don't really analyze your thoughts or feelings?" I ask. "You just report them in an honest manner?"

"True, I don't embellish."

"Just the facts, so to speak," I ascertain.

"And that isn't as easy as it sounds, David. I find that, as time goes by, I have to keep working at it, finding new horizons for my awareness of what's happening within me, as well as around me."

"So it's a process that doesn't get dull or routine," I add.

"Hardly."

5. BLAMELESS PERFORMANCE APPRAISAL

"So, getting back to our leader, Carl, how would that function best be served in terms of our discussion on emotional honesty? What would you say to a novice leader who came to you for advice?"

"I'd say, honesty is most important."

"About?"

"About the basic aspects of each individual's performance. Here's where our behaviorist friends have something to offer—no judgment, no blame, just objective feedback on how something is lacking or could be improved upon, and with a warm smile, with a reassuring demeanor."

6. NO DOWN-LINE HIERARCHY

"So there's not a sense of that 'power over' we were discussing."

"No, more like an equal partner..."

"So in such teams, the boss becomes more like a partner, yet still maintains the higher degree of responsibility . . ."

"The important thing," he continues, "is to make sure the leader is understood. The best way, I imagine, is to have the other person 'play back' what he thinks the leader has said. That will help the leader."

"So the leader can ensure that the team member is digesting what he's hearing bit by bit, however large those bits are, and how much he can handle comfortably at any given time."

"If you mean that the leader makes sure to get feedback on what he says," continues Carl, "then I agree with you. I'm not sure what you mean about the 'bits'."

"What I mean, Carl, is that the leader can focus on one aspect or piece of a job at a time, and gauge how big that piece should be, depending on the ongoing feedback he gets."

"That makes sense, David."

We're ready for the walk back to the car, but not before taking a lingering look at the horizon, as the setting sun, partially covered by a hazy mist along the horizon, creates majestic rays reaching for the heavens.

Just remembering these moments is special for me, consolidating many memories of shared explorations with Carl. His openness encouraged me to be open, and contributes in no small way to my taking on the challenge of writing this book.

If Carl Rogers were alive today, he'd be the first to whom I'd offer the initial draft of this book. On the other hand, at some level, who's to say he wasn't an essential part of the creative process, whether through memory or spiritual presence?

"All I can be is myself," is what Carl taught. That's an aspiration I hold dear to my heart, not always easily accomplished, as he himself admitted.

Wherever you are, Carl, this book is dedicated to you and those you influenced to become more open and authentic. It is dedicated as well to those business leaders who are, as was Carl Rogers, courageous enough to explore the possibilities of putting emotional intelligence to work.

3

The Personal Benefits of Emotional Intelligence

What is it to be wise?
'Tis but to know how little can be known;
To see all others' faults, and feel your own.

—POPE, *Essay on Man*

If you look around yourself at work, I'll bet that you'll find at least some folks who are indisputably intelligent in terms of conventional IQ working under some who are decidedly less intelligent. Chances are great that what the less intelligent superiors have that the more intelligent subordinates lack is *emotional intelligence*.

THE ADVANTAGES OF EMOTIONAL INTELLIGENCE

This chapter outlines the advantages that emotional intelligence provides to allow individuals to succeed, independent of their rational intelligence: self-awareness, the ability to manage emotions, self-motivation, superior management skills and reduction of stress.

Sharpening Your Instincts

Knowing your own feelings on an ongoing basis is key to being sensitive to others' emotions. If you can't identify your own feelings you'll have no basis by which to measure others' feelings. Much of reading others' feelings is through reflection and osmosis. You see the emotional indications in another—a tearing of the eye, a trembling of the lower lip, a flushing of the face— and remember what that felt like when you gave similar indications. Only then can you come close to reading another's feelings. Those who are very sensitive to others' feelings not only remember their own feelings on such occasions—they actually reexperience them. That's why you see people cry at movie theaters or become physically aggressive at soccer matches.

Controlling Your Negative Emotions

In addition, knowing how to label your own feelings gives you at least some sense of control over your life, even when you're highly emotional and vulnerable. For example, if you're feeling highly anxious about a legal or financial problem, you can feel somewhat less anxious by taking the time and having the awareness to label your feelings as "anxiety." Doing so gives you a bit of distance from the sense of helplessness usually accompanying anxiety. By becoming a witness to your own emotion, you create some distance from it, because the "witness" is not as anxious as the "you" before such awareness.

I know this sounds strange if you're new to the idea, so let me elaborate. I, David, feel anxious about a problem. I can't stop my heart from beating hard and fast, even when I go to bed at night. So I decide to become a witness to my anxiety. I identify this uncomfortable feeling as "anxiety" and analyze my problem to figure out what about it is so scary. Then David/witness can objectively look at David/person and articulate the following: "How interesting that David/person is frightened by such-and-such a component of his problem! Of course, he's anxious. I, David/witness would be too, if I were in his shoes. But I'm not. I'm too busy witnessing what's happening with him. How can I comfort him?"

Although this type of dialog may sound a little crazy, this self-observation is the basis of the calming effect of meditation, in which we witness the entity living in our body, going through the trials and tribulations of life, while our meditative self relaxes comfortably and just witnesses.

Other negative emotions such as anger and the sense of failure when things don't work out as planned can also be attenuated by such witnessing. The self-awareness that comes with emotional intelligence allows you to manage negative emotions more effectively and bounce back to your successful, confident self more quickly. This means more productive time and a happier disposition.

Discovering Your Talents and Making Them Work for You

Knowing your own emotional landscape—what triggers your various emotions, especially the most intense ones, when they are triggered, what makes you feel motivated—gives you the perspective you need to arrange the conditions of your life so that you can get motivated when you choose to and stay motivated for as long as you like. Although this is not a 100-percent, foolproof function, it's certainly superior to emotional ignorance.

Knowing what makes you feel good helps to integrate that into your work so that you feel more motivated. For example, as I sit here and write, there is soft music in the background and a cup of delicious coffee on the table. As well, I'm in a setting where I can't be disturbed by callers or the phone. I enjoy this kind of solitude, so I look forward to writing, knowing that I'll get to enjoy the solitude as well.

I also enjoy interacting with people in a helpful way. And so I feel motivated to do my consulting. I don't enjoy the feeling of blowing my own horn, so when it comes to promoting myself, I hire professionals, if necessary. If you enjoy one-on-one interaction, you can build that into your job situation as much as possible. If you don't enjoy one-on-one interaction, you can delegate that function. In either case, you've identified what makes you feel good or bad and have adjusted your work style accordingly, raising your motivation to keep working productively.

Superior Management Skills

Managing others successfully means being able to read their emotions. If you can do that well, you gain others' trust and loyalty, and as a result, their devotion.

Understanding others' emotions is clearly an advantage if you're managing others. You can more easily understand what makes them tick in terms of motivation and in terms of keeping them productive so that they're happy too. If you're in sales or sales training, you can use your ability to read others well as an advantage in finding the right customers and identifying their needs as they relate to your product.

A highly intelligent individual lacking entirely in emotional intelligence would be a very poor manager indeed. Although highly motivated and efficient with his own work, he would tend to be critical of others' work rather than encouraging or helpful, and would probably be uneasy relating to others in any way other than to give instructions in a somewhat cool manner. Others may see him as a cold fish and tend to avoid him. They might describe him in all kinds of negative ways—as manipulative, self-seeking, aloof, uncaring, secretive. The truth of the matter is that none of these labels may be accurate. It's just that this person is totally devoid of emotional intelligence.

INTEGRATING EMOTIONAL INTELLIGENCE INTO YOUR WORKING STYLE

If you want to add emotional intelligence to your rational intelligence to form executive intelligence, consider the following sections in which I'll elaborate on each advantage of executive intelligence and give some tips on how to integrate them into your current working style.

Sharpening Your Instincts

Self-awareness is the keystone of emotional intelligence, around which all of its other characteristics fall—the understanding and effective management of others, more trust in your own feelings, and motivation of self and others.

There are two facets to the function of tuning in to your own feelings:

- Focusing on the feelings themselves and thereby making them easier to recognize, and
- Acknowledging the feelings as in the witnessing process and thereby attenuating them.

These two facets can play off one another, helping you to be more sensitive to positive, healthy feelings by focusing on them, or helping you to decrease or minimize unpleasant emotions, such as distressful anxiety, by categorizing them.

The focusing function is helpful in your efforts to be sensitive to others' feelings, as you experience those feelings yourself through empathy. The labeling function, on the other hand, is helpful in keeping anxiety or gloom from becoming overwhelming. The appropriate interplay of these two opposing functions can help keep you emotionally balanced and productive throughout the workday.

Self-awareness is particularly useful in the process of decision making. Most decisions require more than black-and-white comparisons. If they were that simple, anyone could make them.

Instead, decisions usually involve several dimensions of complexity. Trying to make most decisions with reason alone is not the wisest approach. To the extent that you can include the input of your emotional intelligence, you'll end up with more productive and successful decisions.

If this doesn't happen naturally, you can take time out for emotional introspection. Find a distraction-free environment, relax comfortably and monitor your emotions as you play out the consequences of the various decision options. Then, in addition to the logical outcomes your mind comes up with, you also have your feelings, taking into consideration the much more complex ramifications. It's as if you have the benefit of both digital and analog devices at your service—the digital giving you information on the logical, quantifiable aspects and the analog giving you the overall, qualitative aspects, too complex to be accurately measured. By combining logical and emotional intelligence, you are way ahead of those without the help of their executive intelligence. Self-awareness is clearly a plus, whether in managing others or in complex decision making.

Controlling Your Negative Emotions

It was John's first exposure to executive intelligence as a concept. As he sat in the first row during my talk, eager to challenge this new idea, he seemed troubled. Finally, the elderly CEO spoke up. "David, it's been my experience over the years that emotions can have a disruptive effect in a business setting. Do I understand you correctly to be advocating more rather than less emotion in the work setting?"

I'd heard that question many times before, and was happy to answer it. "No, John, what I'm advocating is the awareness and acknowledgment of emotion, not its expression."

"Good," said John, "because I've been pretty angry a time or two, and I'm glad I didn't give myself the freedom to express it. Somebody might 'a got hurt!"

It used to be thought that venting anger was good for the system, like releasing steam from a pressure cooker. But more current research has revealed that the healthiest response is to acknowledge, that is, admit to, the anger and then to let it go—release it. The earlier in the process anger is recognized, the easier it is to let go of it.

The same is true of frustrations in the workplace. The sooner they can be acknowledged and recognized, the easier it is to change the situation for the better with no grudges held. The key is to learn to identify feelings easily and quickly when appropriate, and then to acknowledge any possibly destructive emotions so they can be either privately witnessed or publicly resolved.

Another emotion to manage is worry. Worry is what happens when we focus on the pessimistic and let our imagination take over, creating anxiety. The anxiety can begin to feed on itself, becoming more and more upsetting.

Here's what I recommend as an emotionally intelligent way to manage worry. First of all, assign a certain time of day to deal with all your worries, let's say 5:30 to 6:00 P.M., or whatever half-hour period you prefer. Then, any time a worry comes up, just say to yourself, "Well, I'll just have to worry about that at my worry-time. This will just have to wait its turn with all my other worries." That gives you a high degree of control over your worries. Instead of giving them free range over the landscape of your emotions, you've corralled them into a half-hour time frame. Like leading a stray sheep into its pen, you can relegate a stray worry to its assigned time frame. And when 5:30 comes along, then you really do worry, but in an emotionally intelligent manner, as follows.

First, analyze each worry to consider whether it's really worth worrying about. If it is, then consider all the options available to you. Then make some phone calls, either to a professional whose expertise would help solve the problem, or to a co-worker or acquaintance who might have the necessary expertise (just like the superstars in the Kelley-Caplan study mentioned in Chapter

7) or can guide you to someone else who might. Then let go of that particular worry, and move on. With this emotionally intelligent approach, you confront worries head-on, leaving the remaining $23^1/_2$ hours worry-free.

The third of the three emotions to manage is depression. There are two types of depression: a reaction to loss and the type with no known cause. In the first case, at least there's some comfort in knowing the cause, but that's usually very small comfort. In this case, there is usually something you can do to help your situation, if not to get rid of your depression, at least to make it slightly less painful.

Using a process known as "cognitive reframing," Shelby Taylor and her associates (1989) had her subjects look at the positive rather than the negative aspects of a loss. For example, if one was transferred to a new job site, instead of saying, "Oh, I'll never find anyone as good as my present neighbors—I'll never enjoy such a great neighborhood again," you might say, "What a bother some of those neighbors were! Remember the time they sent their son over—such an insensitive dolt whom I never did like anyway—and he ate all the food in my fridge, not to mention that he drove that pretty, red car of mine without permission. I'm lucky to be moving so I can be rid of that scoundrel."

If the depression is of unknown cause, it may be even more difficult to manage. Here are four countermeasures you can resort to:

- Exercise, to reduce feelings of passive helplessness and to counteract the depression with the natural high of feeling fit
- Meditation or some form of spiritual or religious participation, to overcome the pain of emotional isolation
- Volunteer work, to help others and to feel nurturing and connected rather than alone
- Medical treatment or psychological counseling

By approaching the three troublesome emotions of anger, anxiety and depression with emotional intelligence, you can be healthier and more productive, and your workplace will experience less absenteeism and more contribution to bottom-line results. As an executive, once you've learned to manage these debilitating emotions in yourself, you can assist your officers and managers to do so as well, fostering their gratitude and devotion. If you don't end up working happily ever after together, at least you'll be a quantum leap ahead of your competitors who struggle on in emotional ignorance.

Discovering Your Talents and Making Them Work for You

Knowing your own emotions helps to fine-tune your work style so that you can integrate whatever makes you feel good into your work. Beyond that, there is another type of self-awareness that helps you to determine the components of your job at which you excel. You can sense this by the good feeling you have when you are most involved in a particular component of your work—be it analyzing a plan, training a group or resolving a conflict. Whatever you enjoy the most is probably also what you're best at. Ironically, this is the specific skill you should spend most of your free time fine-tuning. This is your talent; to make it your cutting edge, you should keep improving it over time, for this talent will be your key to success as time goes by. It's what can separate you from the rest when promotion decisions are to be made.

Even though you already enjoy and excel at a particular part of your job, continue to improve on it not just by taking on more challenges in that area, but also by reading about it, practicing it off the job whenever possible, making it part of a hobby or volunteer opportunity. If you enjoy financial analysis or training or conflict resolution, you can read more about these, including biographies of those who are proven masters; you can teach noncredit courses in these areas; you can volunteer your services to community organizations, seeking new challenges for your growing talent. Any of these will give you that cutting edge of superior performance when promotional decisions are made.

The famous marshmallow study begun by Walter Mischel and his associates in the 1960s (see Shoda, Mischel, and Peake, 1990), in which 4-year-olds were offered a second marshmallow if they could resist the impulse to eat the first one for about 5 or so minutes, is a milestone in the research of emotional intelligence. The children who resisted the initial impulse and waited for the second treat, when tested over a decade later, were found to be more assertive, less easily frustrated and more adept at personal relations. Moreover, they were better students.

The characteristic identified here, and one that is so crucial in success in the business world, as elsewhere, is known as "delayed gratification," the ability to put off immediate satisfaction for later benefit, to work hard today for tomorrow's success, to invest now for future wealth. This is the stuff from which success is honed. It should be made clear here that putting aside present pleasure and focusing on the future is not the same as worry. In fact, delayed gratification is, in a sense, the opposite of worry. Delayed gratification is hopeful and optimistic. Worry, on the other hand, is despairing and pessimistic.

Worry is not only nonproductive; it's actually destructive. It can affect your judgment and disturb your concentration. But now you have some techniques to help you overcome worry. At this point, I want to explore a very important facet of self-motivation—how to enjoy the most intense aspect of your work.

Mihaly Csikszentmihaly, in his book *Flow* (1990), describes the best work an individual can do as an ecstatic flow of experience. For two decades, he studied men and women doing the work they most enjoyed and asked them what it felt like.

Doing the best you can and letting yourself get totally caught up in it so that you actually lose track of time is what the ecstatic flow of work is all about. According to Csikszentmihaly, the more you focus on the intensity of work you enjoy, the more creative and productive you can be. So practice and fine tune your talents and then enjoy the heck out of them! What a great discovery for self-motivation!

Superior Management Skills

The CEOs of yesteryear rarely smiled. As a matter of fact, you could almost tell a person's status by how rarely she smiled. The higher up in the hierarchy, the more stone-faced the demeanor. Today's emotionally intelligent CEO presents a much brighter picture. She's more likely to be a good communicator and a warm, caring figure, as well as popular and charismatic.

The emotionally intelligent executive knows how to create instant rapport with practically anyone. She's confident, self-assured, and feels comfortable adapting to many personal styles. Yet, as adaptable as she is, she can set the tone when that's called for.

The tone of the emotionally intelligent executive is set by speaking directly, forthrightly, clearly, and most importantly, when appropriate. Timing is of the essence. Most of the time, listening should come before speaking. Then the executive can be more focused on the issue at hand, with the appropriate degree of intensity. She can be forceful when necessary and emanate a sense of trustworthiness and know-how. In many cases, she demonstrates excellent platform skills.

In addition to being able to read others' feelings well and to express a warmly supportive personality, emotionally intelligent executives have two other abilities—to mediate effectively between opposing factions, and to organize individuals into an effective team effort.

Not only can they read others' feelings well, but emotionally intelligent executives are also quite adept at reading the unspoken, collective feelings of the teams they oversee, and can articulate what they sense. Like successful politicians, they make their staff members, both individually and collectively, feel appreciated and supported. They radiate warmth and acceptance.

As I've mentioned, it's much easier to read others' feelings when you can identify your own clearly. Research has shown that information processing is more accurate with emotional openness. The more you can "step into another's shoes," emotionally speaking, the more you'll understand that person's perspective and the better the communication overall. When team members are fully tuned to one another, they function together most harmoniously.

Emotionally intelligent executives can engage in delayed gratification in terms of temporarily setting aside their own emotional needs in order to portray what they sense to be most propitious for particular group interactions. At such times, their sensitivity to group sensibilities overrides their own need for self-expression. They are devoted to maintaining the integrity of the teams' expectations of their officers, rather than to any discordant expression of their own.

If my description of an emotionally intelligent executive sounds formulaic, I should add the following caveats:

- It's all in the timing.
- Don't let yourself get out of touch.

Let me explain.

Taking the role of leadership in the manner I've just described is highly sensitive to the matter of timing. If you're forced to take responsibility for management, even in an emotionally intelligent manner, too quickly, you may be setting yourself up for failure. Assuming leadership, before you have a good sense of the group feeling of those you're to manage, may well result in failure.

Politicians prove their mettle by "pressing flesh," or meeting as many of their would-be constituents as they can on a one-to-one basis—smiling, kissing babies, but also collecting information. They can subsequently convey in public speeches and telecasts that they have a good grasp on the people's feelings and expectations. If they're more accurate in their reading of public feeling than their opponents, they'll be elected to office (other things being equal).

In a business setting, this reading of the people is also very helpful, and just as essential as it is in politics. On the other hand, the timing factor is more important in business than in politics. In politics, efforts are generally focused in a limited timeframe, such as an election. In business, it takes a growing sense of trust and confidence based on a history of accurate judgment calls and emotionally intelligent communication skills. Such skills are not acquired overnight or simply by reading about them in this book. They're acquired gradually through experience and conscientious and sincere effort.

"Wannabe" managers who politically maneuver their way into position or who use family connections to accelerate their careers unfairly are likely to meet with strong resistance from their subordinates. If such "politicians" or protégés are out of touch with their staff members and consistently make unpopular decisions that prove financially unwise as well, they're doomed to failure, unless they're kept in place because of their connections. No matter what the organizational chart signifies, the subordinates may rebel.

There's no skirting the fact that before a manager can successfully assume that role, a certain degree of emotional intelligence is required:

- To be able to read the staff's collective personality, and this can only be done with intent and over time.
- To convey this sensitivity to the group, and that takes a certain degree of authenticity, because groups detect phoniness more easily than do most individuals.
- To wait until the group is ready for the new manager, and this takes delayed gratification.

Observe, communicate, and only then, get set to manage from a position of strength, with executive intelligence.

Decreasing Absenteeism

The stressed-out worker will miss more days at the office, whether for reasons of true illness or just to escape from pressure. Stress takes its toll physiologically, through the oversecretion of hormones such as adrenaline, prolactin and cortisol, which results in a weaker immune system and/or a decrease in or downright absence of productive energy. Stress puts the physiology of the body at high alert and drains that physiological component that ordinarily maintains the immune system.

In addition, poor communication skills in the workplace can lead to frustrations resulting in chronic anger. If this chronic anger persists long enough, it can result not only in heart disease, but in death at a younger age. According to Dr. John Barefoot at University of North Carolina, the severity of coronary heart disease is in direct relation to results on tests of hostility. This was reported by his colleague, Dr. Redford Williams at Duke University, who found that doctors scoring high on hostility while in medical school were seven times more likely to die by age 50 than those scoring low (Williams, 1989). In other words, ongoing anger can not only increase absenteeism, it can even result in early death. Absenteeism due to heart attack can be long-lasting; that due to death is permanent.

As a matter of fact, the Japanese have identified a syndrome of sudden death due to overwork called *karoshi*. In Japanese workers, psychosomatic disorders are often the consequence of competitive and demanding work. According to Akiri Ikemi of Okayama University and Shinya Kubota of the University of Occupational and Environmental Health in Japan,

> In work as a lifelong commitment, human relationships are extremely delicate, despite the intense competition . . . Moreover, decisions are often made collectively, and it is the manager's responsibility to listen to and foster the opinion of workers . . . the manager plays more the role of the facilitator . . . In short, it is vital for managers to listen and to understand the worker as a person. The

very problem is that they lack the adequate training and knowledge to do so. (1996, p. 107)

Japanese managers are culturally set up to act as emotionally intelligent managers but without the requisite skills. No wonder a number of them end up with sickness and early deaths. Beginning in 1988, Ikemi and Kubota set up 5-day programs to teach Japanese corporate executives the skills of "experiential listening," "listening to the felt sense," and "focusing/listening," all of which I'm sure fit neatly into our understanding of emotionally intelligent management.

Their guidelines for better listening skills involve five steps:

1. Have eye contact with the speaker.
2. Don't cut off statements.
3. Respond genuinely.
4. Understand the process, not only conclusions.
5. Don't impose your own view, but listen responsively to develop the speaker's own conclusions. (1996, pp. 114–115)

The results were that workers looked at one another when speaking, they were able to feel what was being said, they were more honest, the speakers felt understood, information was communicated more effectively. Managers were less likely to impose their views just because of their status. Everyone felt more appreciated, creative ideas flourished, conflict diminished. These changes were nothing short of miraculous given the hierarchical nature of Japanese society. To quote Ikemi and Kubota,

> When interviewed, staff members said that informal communication between staff and manager was unheard of in this department with the exception of a couple of occasions a year (e.g., the New Year's party), and, at times, even those conversations were like those "between a feudal king and a peasant." Workers felt happy to know that their supervisor was making efforts to understand them as persons. (1996, p. 117)

As a result of such efforts, illness among workers was reduced, and so was absenteeism. Workers who were considering leaving their employ reconsidered after the new training was completed. Most clearly, the incidents of fatigue, depression and anxiety of over 1,600 workers were significantly lowered, as reported in a statistical analysis. Emotional intelligence reduces stress and absenteeism not only in our culture but in others as well.

It seems quite clear that one of the benefits of working in an emotionally intelligent environment is the reduction of stress and frustration. With better communication of support and more disclosure of authentic feelings, there is less to be stressed or angry about. With less stress and frustration there is not only the prospect of healthier hearts, but also of fewer ulcer problems, fewer colds, fewer asthma attacks, fewer cases of diabetes onset and superior memory functions, according to a research review by Bruce McEwen and Eliot Stellar (1993).

Just having a socially supportive environment seems to result in less stress and better health. According to a 1982 research article by D. G. Blazer, people who feel socially isolated are more likely to get sick or die than those who feel emotionally supported.

This is not to say that workers need to have someone around all the time holding their hand. What is important is to have the *sense* that support is at hand, not necessarily that they have others physically present. It is not being alone that causes stress, but rather the vulnerable *feeling* of aloneness and the threats to one's ongoing life status. Such threats as feeling insecure at work, possibly due to interpersonal conflict, and the resulting fear of financial precariousness due to job insecurity, if sufficiently chronic, severe, and cumulative, can lead to early death, according to a 1993 article in the *British Medical Journal* (Rosengren, 1993).

One way of establishing a sense of support is through sharing one's troubles with a trusting associate. Somehow, unburdening oneself is healthy for the heart. Ludwig van Beethoven, better known for his music, wrote the following in 1817:

Evil is mysterious and appears greatest when viewed in solitude. Discussed with others, it seems more endurable because one becomes entirely familiar with that which we dread and feel it has been overcome. (Ryback, 1996)

Over a century and a half later, psychologist James Pennebaker (1992) came up with a similar conclusion, more scientifically based. When he had people write about their most traumatic experiences, he found that the result was an enhanced immune function and a drop in absenteeism. The healthiest pattern, according to Dr. Pennebaker, was when these individuals expressed the intensity of their emotions first, followed by a meaningful account of the traumatic story itself.

The need to reduce anger, worry, and anxiety in the workplace seems a foregone conclusion. Without such reduction of these destructive and uncomfortable emotions, the immune system is compromised and absenteeism rises with increased incidents of illness.

One of the most dramatic findings of emotional support as an aid to longer life came from survivors of breast cancer. Dr. David Spiegel found that, when survivors of advanced metastatic breast cancer went to weekly support groups where one "becomes entirely familiar with that which we dread" (to use Beethoven's words), they lived twice as long, on the average, as those survivors who remained with their problems "viewed in solitude." The women going to the weekly groups lived, on the average, 37 months after initial treatment; those going it alone lived only 19 months longer (Spiegel, et al., 1989).

There is clearly a connection between the felt sense of emotional support and better health. In the workplace, this translates to an emotionally intelligent environment resulting in a reduction in absenteeism. Study after study has confirmed this.

CONCLUSION

Emotional intelligence can be a benefit at home as well as at the workplace. A deeper and more appreciative understanding of family and friends, less stressful emotions, avoidance of worry, better listening skills and improved health are all benefits of an emotionally intelligent lifestyle. Although the benefits are great, a gradual approach to taking on a new lifestyle is better than biting off more than one can chew at any given time period. Changes in interpersonal attitude can be challenging to those at the receiving end, so sensitivity is necessary here as well. Although the prospects of great benefit are exciting, "easy does it" is the best approach.

In the next chapter, we'll take a closer look at moving executives from a formal, hierarchical structure to the diametrically opposed emotional intelligence form of management and see why it has become important at this point.

4

Emotions in the Workplace— Then and Now

> On the basis of my experience I have found that if I can help
> bring about a climate marked by genuineness, prizing, and
> understanding, then exciting things happen. Persons and
> groups in such a climate move away from rigidity and toward
> flexibility, away from static living toward process living, away
> from dependence toward self-acceptance, away from being
> predictable toward an unpredictable creativity.
>
> —CARL ROGERS, *A Way of Being*

If emotions can be so uncomfortable, then how can we make them fit when they're first introduced into the workplace? Another question: How do we deal with heavy emotions in the workplace that impose themselves over us rather than support us?

Emotions are much, much older than intellect. When we ask if our cats or dogs have emotions, we're asking the wrong question. There's no doubt that our pets have emotions. What they may or may not have is sufficient reason and memory to use their emotions in ways that make sense to us, their human companions.

THE PURPOSE OF EMOTIONS—THEN AND NOW

Our prehistoric ancestors used their emotions: They used fear to survive, joy to bond with one another, anger to help defend their territories (physical and psychological), love to procreate.

In the twenty-first-century workplace, emotions can be used in a different way—to clarify intent, to consolidate bonds of supportive teamwork, to motivate, and, not least, to bring personal meaning into the hours spent in our working day.

In past generations, the recognition of emotion in the workplace was suspect. Today, it is essential. The emotions we can use in the workplace today are not the raw passions of fear, greed and rage, but rather the tamer, communicative emotions that help us articulate more clearly our concerns about our customers' personalities, about our interactions with other competitors, about our capability to accomplish the emerging goals set before us in self-managed teams. It is our emotional awareness that is productive, not the raw expression of passion.

The autocratic captains of industry of yesteryear are "dinosaurs" in the current business environment. In today's business world, there is so much dependence on the knowledge factor, on communication skills, and on team effort, that it is difficult if not impossible for a single individual to carry the crux of responsibility without support from others. What is needed today is emotional intelligence.

EMOTIONAL INTELLIGENCE = EMOTIONS + AWARENESS

Emotional intelligence integrates awareness of our emotions with intellectual knowledge of the world around us. In Freudian terms, emotional intelligence combines the conscious ego with the unconscious, even more authentic, id. The function of emotional intelligence could be compared to the function of sonar on a ship: It provides a more total picture of the situation, and helps avoid unseen obstacles and problems. Just as the ship's captain can see only above the surface of the water, and sonar provides information about the underwater landscape, emotional intelligence in the workplace helps us see what our logic may overlook and helps us to steer the best, safest course to business success. Before we were aware of the concept of emotional intelligence, this would be referred to as a "gut feeling."

Emotional intelligence is best defined as the ability to use your awareness and sensitivity to discern the feelings underlying interpersonal communication, and to resist the temptation to respond impulsively and thoughtlessly, but instead to act from receptivity, authenticity and candor. The term "executive intelligence" has all of these characteristics of emotional intelligence, but within the business-oriented context, including such factors as profitability, marketability, personnel and current company policy. In other words, executive intelligence is the use of emotional intelligence in the business context, taking into consideration all the necessary and appropriate factors leading to satisfactory and productive decision making. At times, I will use the terms interchangeably.

EMOTION ENHANCES MEMORY

Do you remember what you were doing on a particular day—let's say, November 22, 1963? If you're over 40 years old, then you most likely do, for that was the day of President Kennedy's assassination at 12:30 P.M. Central time, as he rode in an open limousine through Dallas, Texas. Or perhaps you remember what you were doing on that fateful day when Challenger exploded in the sky in January 1986. I had just gotten through showering after a workout, just in time to see the drama unfold on television.

I mention this to illustrate how important emotions can be in the process of memory. We usually think of memory as a purely intellectual function, yet the ease with which we remember something is directly proportional to its meaning and the emotion it arouses in us. The assassination of a president arouses strong emotions in nearly everyone, so we remember what we were doing when we heard the terrible news. However, except for those with extraordinary recall, few have any idea what they were doing the day before the assassination or the Challenger incident.

The more we find our work emotionally meaningful through shared, supportive, open communication, the more we can learn and remember about our work and the more effectively we can apply ourselves to it. The end result for the organization, because it uses its members' minds more productively, is a higher profit statement, the main goal of any for-profit commercial enterprise.

A BALANCING ACT

It is true that emotions are not easily quantified and often feel overwhelming and out of control. That's precisely why those who fear emotions in the workplace often feel so stressed. As I said earlier, emotional intelligence focuses not so much on the expression of emotions as on emotional awareness, sensitivity, and insight.

Perhaps because emotions played such a great role in our forebears' survival, our emotions can detect threat more quickly and more sensitively than can our intellect alone. Sometimes our emotions overreact and suspect threat where it doesn't really exist. In extreme cases, others can see us as paranoid. One of the effects of emotional support in the workplace is to counteract such irrational and inappropriate fears. Ideally, the sensitivity that comes with emotional intelligence is buffered by the support that also comes with it.

The irony of emotion in the workplace is that, in the "strong, silent" values of past generations, intense emotions of anxiety and rage due to frustration could often interfere with effective logical process. In the modern era, however, the support that comes with emotional intelligence can foster a more productive logical process. This is especially essential to self-managed groups, creating an aura of self-confidence. External threat can then be gauged more accurately and dealt with more appropriately.

At its best, executive intelligence allows for balanced interaction between intellect and emotion in the workplace so that emotional awareness fine-tunes decision making on a moment-to-moment basis. Like a well-rehearsed tango between practiced partners, intellect and emotion play and work hand-in-hand, so that neither dominates the other. Rather, at any given moment, both will have about equal input.

WHY EXECUTIVE INTELLIGENCE NOW?

Why is executive emotional intelligence so important for success in business at this point in history? The answer has to do with the shifting pace—the exhilarating acceleration of change in business, the revolution from objects to information, from the industrial age to the electronic age, from the prevalence of machines to the priority of knowledge.

In preindustrial days many jobs could be initiated, executed and finalized by an individual. The cobbler, butcher, or black-smith set up shop, marketed through word of mouth, did all their own work, billed and collected and even paid the tax man. If they were successful, they might acquire an apprentice or two, but most were essentially one-man operations.

That is hardly possible these days, except for professionals and consultants, and even these typically work in groups. The cobbler has given way to the factory, the butcher to the processing plant and the smith to the ironworks. In the modern workplace, factories, plants and organizations have superseded the lone worker.

In the past few decades, as we've begun to focus on the competitive edge of added value, the final product or service has been subject to improvement through fine-tuning the collective process. Each individual's contribution has become an integral component of the final product, made superior by special effort at each step of the process. As we enter the twenty-first century, the focus on team effort becomes paramount.

Such collaboration makes the communication process more crucial than ever. Most essential is the customer's perspective, which gives direction for fine-tuning the components that feed into the final product, and helps gain the cutting edge at the point of purchase. Each contributor to the process needs to know how all the facets fit together to win the customer's dollar vote.

Distribution used to refer to the process of trucks delivering merchandise over interstate highways. Now it means communicating data over the information superhighway. The speed limit is no longer 55 or 70 miles per hour; it's virtually the speed of light. While we were busy watching the Berlin Wall come down and adjusting to becoming middle-aged baby-boomers, an information revolution quietly snuck by us.

Intelligence is now more essential than ever—not the intelligence of a Vietnam-era McNamara peeling off body counts with the accuracy of a calculator, but rather the deeper intelligence that understands people at their most basic, complex and humane levels. This emotional intelligence includes the ability to reach beyond the persona of your staff members, beyond their defenses, beyond the obvious, and to understand the deeper feelings that determine human behavior in the workplace. It means controlling your own impulses to react out of greed or lust or fear, to have the inner discipline to hear what is being communicated most deeply, and only then to respond with intent and integrity, mindful of the long-term effect rather than quick and easy profit, to try to understand *why* your associates are doing what they're doing, beyond superficial appearance.

The industrial revolution took place in the nineteenth century, when machines made factory labor possible and profitable, and people migrated from the countryside to teeming cities to enjoy the new demand for workers. The information revolution is less obvious; it is a more "inner" revolution, a change in how people communicate, how production is planned and executed. The change can been seen in the way marketing is becoming inextricably linked with demographics, and in how the five continents of our planet have become an interconnected network of instantaneous interaction. The only sensible response to all this challenging turmoil is the ability to think quickly and accurately about human behavior—putting emotional intelligence to work.

BUSINESS IN THE INFORMATION REVOLUTION

During the industrial revolution, business operated in a hierarchical fashion. Factories were run by directors of operations, who were bosses of managers, who were responsible for supervisors. The chain of command was sacrosanct. Although such structure still exists today, those most successful at facing the information revolution are experimenting with new forms of self-management. Response time needs to be quicker, and an understanding of people's emotional responses is more important than ever. The consumer, with increasing access to computer technology, has become more demanding and more service oriented, looking for good business relationships in an otherwise cynical world.

In order to react more quickly, companies are feeling more pressure to decentralize, to allow decisions to be made closer to the point of the problem, to allow emotional intelligence to determine the most appropriate solution. The smaller the loop of communication, the better. Two people can respond more quickly than 10 or 50, or a hierarchy of 1,000. With emotional intelligence, a small group decision can be as effective as one making its snail-paced movement through the hierarchy, yet fast enough to compete in a twenty-first-century hyper-communication marketplace. The rigid and formal chain of command is no longer competitive.

So change is necessary, but at an emotionally intelligent pace. Now, more than ever, intelligent decisions are crucial to survival. Quick response at a point most proximal to the problem is called for, and more people trained in executive intelligence to be available for such response. In other words, we need less hierarchy and more self-management.

This means that virtually every individual in the organization can become a surrogate entrepreneur, one with the emotional intelligence to act independently and with the larger picture clearly in mind. Such a well-trained individual can initiate responses, obtain support from associates as needed and document the outcome. Emotional intelligence provides flexibility—human nature is the same no matter what the specific problem. The client/customer inevitably demands to be treated with warmth and understanding. If one company won't provide these, another will. Companies without the empowerment dynamics of executive intelligence will fail; those with it will succeed.

EMOTIONAL INTROSPECTION?

The old Cartesian duality of mind and body (first put forth by the seventeenth-century French philosopher, René Descartes)—or intellect and emotion in our frame of reference—no longer holds. This dualistic thinking is what has kept emotions under wraps in the workplace. Emotion and intellect are better seen as paired in a combination that enhances intellect to a more successful level of application than if it were isolated from emotion.

Even Richard Herrnstein and Charles Murray, authors of *The Bell Curve* (1994), agree that IQ by itself is not a good predictor of success in an individual's life. Much more important, they say, is "the totality of other characteristics that he brings to life" (p. 66).

The other characteristics might easily be, at least in part, those of emotional intelligence, such as motivation, insight as to what will work in the long run, the skill of garnering emotional support to keep destructive emotions resolved and long-range planning based on deep values recognized through emotional introspection.

The term "emotional introspection" at first sounds like an oxymoron. "Introspection" can be seen as referring to inner intellectual analysis, devoid of emotion. But the term as I'm using it here is akin to meditating on a decision in order to get a clear sense of what emotions arise out of either side of the decision. That way, you can know not only the "dollars and cents," or more practical, consequences of the decision, but also the more sensitive emotional parameters, which take into consideration so many more factors—emotional comfort, social ramifications, ethics, long-term vs. short-term effects, and so on.

As you can see more clearly now, emotional intelligence brings to the workplace not necessarily more expression of intense emotion, but rather the calming, soothing, yet deeper awareness of the elements of the decision-making process itself.

LEARNING THE NEW LANGUAGE OF EMOTION

There are at least two benefits to emotional openness in the workplace—the disclosure of feelings about oneself, such as self-confidence in one's ability to complete a task or to work productively with others and, second, the authentic support of others as they share productive ideas to be considered in the process of brainstorming. If any intense negative emotions do arise, they are acknowledged honestly but are not typically expressed aggressively.

Imagine, for example, a team meeting in which emotional intelligence is being considered for the first time. Apprehension is high. Who discloses what? How much? "What if I share that vulnerability—won't I look stupid?" "This doesn't feel natural," many may think. "I wish I could leave and go home to my family where I can be back in control."

It's like learning a new, unspoken point of view, communicated as much by body language as with words. It's certainly going to be awkward in the beginning. Whoever said change is easy, anyway, especially deep change?

But the end results are worth the effort. Learning this new emotional language is a major step toward becoming emotionally intelligent. And being emotionally intelligent ultimately means a happier work force, greater productivity and higher profits.

THE CARDINAL RULE OF EXECUTIVE INTELLIGENCE: BE HONEST

The cardinal rule in creating an emotionally intelligent business is quite simple and old-fashioned: Always tell the truth. Up to 95 percent of all management problems can thus be more easily solved. From this it follows that people will do what they say they will do and that no cheating or sidestepping will take place. Of course, the truth is not always obvious, even to those who hope to proclaim it. Too many of us feel we don't really know our deeper truths all that clearly. Knowing our deeper self is a special, admirable trait that takes intention and focus over time.

Executive intelligence starts with basic honesty, starting with one's own self-doubts and personal revelations. From this point, honesty about other business matters follows. I wish I could claim to be the first to write this, but someone beat me to the punch—a consultant by the name of Bill Shakespeare: "To thine own self be true, and it must follow, as the night the day, thou canst not then be false to any man" (Hamlet, Act 1, Scene 3).

Being honest with clients and customers means a greater sense of loyalty to them. Ultimately, this will mean better customer relations. It also means taking more initiative to satisfy the client/customer. Sensing the customer's needs, the emotionally intelligent individual sees that these needs are met directly and quickly. All this takes an ongoing effort to stay abreast of the existing technology of your special area so that you can react quickly and efficiently. You can benefit by making the effort to stay informed of your customers' needs on a general basis, to better prepare yourself for the specific situations. Putting emotional intelligence to work entails a continued interest in self-improvement and learning. This is the price of success and fulfillment, whether it takes place in a classroom setting or in the easy chair of your own living room.

Ultimately, emotions and self-management are inextricably tied to one another because it is emotionally intelligent openness that reveals the deeper talents and inner integrity within all individuals that allows for effective, self-managed teamwork. Instead of status based on hierarchy, pride is based on skill and accomplishment. Instead of delegated assignments, there is individual initiative. Instead of competition, there is mutual support and cooperation of complementary skills. Instead of defending "personal territory," there is team coherence in focusing on shared goals of satisfying customers and increasing well-earned profits. Instead of greed, there is integrity. Instead of the labor-intensive Puritan work ethic, there's the New Team Ethic, with personal meaning fueling richer results, in terms of both a meaningful lifestyle and also financial success. As the industrial revolution evolves into the information revolution, the effective integration of emotional sensitivity with self-management brings the New Team Ethic to the forefront.

Now let me share with you what I mean by the "New Team Ethic" . . .

5

The New Team Ethic

We win because we hire the smartest people. We improve our products based on feedback, until they're the best. We have retreats each year where we think about where the world is heading.

—BILL GATES

Peter Drucker coined the term "knowledge worker," referring to those who add to the body of knowledge about business. Writing in the November 1994 issue of *The Atlantic Monthly*, he points out that such individuals are productive as team members rather than as lone contributors. The analyst's efforts, for example, are useless until they are described by the writer whose descriptions are also useless until applied by a computer programmer. It is this combined effort that adds value. Without any one of the three components, the information wouldn't be available to the consumer. This example can be seen as a metaphor for almost all contributions in the workplace. More and more, in our increasingly sophisticated world, we work in teams rather than as individuals.

Under the New Team Ethic, you can get ahead and increase your earning potential by becoming more in tune with your associates, your staff members and your superiors. By knowing what's going on in the hearts as well as the minds of these individuals, you will be able to communicate more effectively and consequently develop a teamwork approach that accomplishes goals more efficiently and with less effort.

The New Team Ethic shifts the focus from the individual decision maker to the self-managed group. Instead of relying only on your own perspective to make executive decisions, you can now have a focus enriched by those with whom you work, whether they be superiors, staff members or associates.

BENEFITS OF THE NEW TEAM ETHIC

From a management point of view, the end result of the New Team Ethic will be a team with less conflict, a greater sense of mutual support, more cooperation and enhanced communication skills. Even more, those in your self-managed teams will have a better understanding of their roles in achieving goals, a stronger sense of being appreciated, and greater comfort in the informal communication process so essential for integrating the unique skills of various team members. Even more, team members in the New Team Ethic will be less hampered by absenteeism—they will be better able to handle personal problems that might otherwise result in debilitating anxiety and medical problems. There will be a natural evolution of company loyalty. Participants feel so good about their accomplishments and their respective individual roles in such accomplishments that they will naturally feel better about their superiors and the company itself. More innovative ideas will lead to more profitable enterprises. A greater sense of integrity and ethics overall will result in fewer threats of litigation. In the end, not only will the individual team members work more effectively and feel more appreciated, but the bottom line of company profits will also benefit substantially. Does this sound too good to be true? Read on . . .

FIVE PRINCIPLES OF THE NEW TEAM ETHIC

The New Team Ethic involves five dynamic interactive principles, which I've developed over years of consulting:

1. Building trusting relationships and effective communication through risk-taking openness, effective listening skills and learning to respect differences of opinion while building on a consensus that proves worthwhile.

2. Creative innovation through group discussions that foster openness and playful opposition.

3. Fostering a sense of self-appreciation and team pride through group discussion focused on patterns of successful decision making and appropriate actions based on emotional insights.

4. Learning to distinguish between decisions based on fact and those based on emotion, as well as the most effective balance between the two for each particular individual.

5. Reducing stress through the encouragement of healthy fitness habits and relaxation techniques.

I'm sure you'll agree this is quite a personal approach to business. However, I assure you that all this unconventional, risky behavior will pay off. Of course, this assumes that the organization already has clear focus, knowledgable and skilled personnel, good goals and measurement systems.

DOUBTING THOMASES

If you're skeptical about the value of emotional sharing in the workplace, you're not alone. Interviewing 250 corporate executives, Michael Maccoby (1976) found they were highly concerned that feeling compassion or empathy at work would put them at odds with company goals and values. One went so far as to claim that doing so would make it "impossible to deal with people."

Many of the others felt that making businesslike decisions would be even more difficult when feelings were given too much consideration.

Although this sentiment was stronger in the past, it prevails among many in today's corporate culture. The business world is still seen by many as a cutthroat environment where might is right. For most, emotions are to be downplayed in the business world, except to manipulate and control others.

MORE POSITIVE, LESS NEGATIVE

For a growing group of foresighted pioneers, however, emotional sensitivity is becoming an increasingly valued commodity in the workplace. More and more, as we prepare to enter the twenty-first century, leadership is seen as a psychological process of building management by consensus using enhanced communication skills. As a consultant with top management, one of the assets I bring to bear in offering my services is the caring and support with which I can deliver the "bad news." It's easy to tell someone, "In my professional opinion, you don't carry your weight!" It takes a bit more thoughtfulness and concern to look at what each individual has to offer in terms of that individual's personal and career histories and the set of limitations and liabilities that go along with them. Assuming each individual has a role to play in our complex business world, I choose my words carefully. "In my opinion, you'd more than carry your weight if you could . . ." and fill in the blank with the direction I consider most apt for that particular individual.

Hearing positive feedback as opposed to criticism makes an incredible difference. Criticism when not buoyed by constructive support can devastate self-esteem and, in extreme cases, even debilitate someone for a day or more. The more the individual receiving the feedback feels capable, the more devastating feedback laden with criticism can be. An individual who feels capable is thrown for a loop when feedback flies in the face of their self-perception.

Just as a glass can be seen as half empty or half full, feedback can be delivered to show something lacking or something to be added. An emotionally intelligent approach takes into consideration the psychological impact of the feedback and avoids negatively toned language. With the compassionate approach the end result, hopefully, is a highly motivated worker eager to take on a different challenge or the same challenge with a different approach. This is a much happier outcome than a disgruntled, depressed worker suffering from a sense of personal failure.

In order to fill in the blank of my recommendation, however, I have to do some homework. I have to acquire some depth of knowledge of the individual to know his strengths and weaknesses and the potential for growth in whatever direction. This is a large part of what the New Team Ethic encourages. In a sense, it allows us all to become consultants to one another.

To the extent that I can really be present for another, that I can really bring myself to care and to feel genuinely supportive of that individual and the organization of which she is a part, I can assist that individual in being a positive contribution to the overall effort. If you doubt this approach, consider the alternative. Adversarial feedback will only deteriorate relations with a problematic employee. A supportive approach will offer the best hope of transforming a negative situation into a positive outcome.

In a study of over 100 managers and white-collar workers, Robert Baron (1990) found that negative or critical feedback was considered a greater source of conflict and frustration than disputes over power, mistrust or personality struggles. Those who were ineptly criticized felt discouraged, demoralized and demotivated. A supportive form of quick feedback would most assuredly have left them encouraged, emotionally uplifted and more highly motivated. Is there any doubt which approach is to be preferred?

Supportive feedback requires not only a depth of knowledge about the individual—knowing how she really feels inside and what she enjoys doing most, among other things—but also knowledge about the job challenge at hand. It's important to know enough about it to consider which aspects of the job are being successfully accomplished, and which are not. Unless feedback is specific in terms of job components, it won't be constructive. Exactly what is being done poorly? Exactly what is being done satisfactorily? And exactly what could be modified to enhance the individual's productivity?

USING TEAM INTELLIGENCE

Just as understanding the dynamics of an individual's work experience can enhance personal productivity, asking the right questions about the marketplace allows for better solutions there, too. The eminent consultant guru, Peter Drucker, in a recent book (1995), points out how such ex-giants as IBM and Kmart have failed by asking the wrong questions. It was their failure to understand the dynamics of the marketplace that led to their failure more than anything else. "How much will the market pay?" was the wrong question. It would have been more fruitful to ask, "What price should we charge for our products in order to ensure that we survive in the long run?"

More and more, survival in today's marketplace is a function of asking the right questions rather than having the right answers to outmoded questions. It takes much more thoughtfulness and insight to survive in today's business world than it did decades ago, years ago, or even six months ago in some industries. Such thoughtfulness can best be achieved through consensual "brain trusts" or enhanced communication among high-level managers and other corporate leaders.

The New Team Ethic promotes such a consensual thinking process by lowering the barriers to creative output, for both individuals and groups. This is fostered by group support garnered over time through the encouragement of open sharing of feelings and opinions within each self-managed group. The end result is a cumulative intelligence of all the conferring brains, but only if the emotional barriers are lowered sufficiently to foster a truly free flow of ideas.

As we become more reliant on high-tech communication modalities—faxes, e-mail, teleconferencing—it becomes more obvious that communication skills are increasingly essential. We no longer have as much luxury to "compose" a letter. We're challenged to communicate in the virtual instant. We can no longer hide behind the cool light of reason when our passions might be raging, be they the terror of anxiety or angry aggression. We must communicate close to "real time" with little opportunity to sleep on decisions before they must be made. The New Team Ethic allows us to deal with our feelings on an ongoing basis rather than storing them up. It allows us to combine intellect and passion in an ongoing manner, rather than letting us become slaves to erupting emotions as we try in vain to suppress them.

CONCLUSION

It hardly needs saying that a group that communicates more effectively will be more productive, yet, till recently, little attention has been paid to this fact. Now, with the increasing respect for the concept of emotional intelligence, more focus on this aspect of productivity will help us overcome the old autocratic modes of conducting business. Emotionally intelligent survivors in this challenging economy will look back with poignant sympathy on the autocratic dinosaurs who contributed to the failures of the economic giants of yesteryear.

In Part II, we'll look at how emotional intelligence got started, what it can mean to you and examine some of its basic assumptions in the workplace.

Part II
What Is Emotional Intelligence?

Ahead of us a boy plays with his two frolicking German shepherds, retrieving the sticks he tosses out. We slow our pace to take in the joy of their game. As we resume our usual pace, Carl is deep in thought. Then he raises his arm, catching my attention. He's ready to share something he's just formulated.

> "If I had anything to do with it, being a good boss would mean devoting some time to finding out the learning needs of the employee. What is it that he needs to know to make him more effective as a worker? A real practical approach, not theory. And then I'd have the boss arrange the working conditions so he could learn what he needs."
>
> "You mean like arranging for him to do something new and then rewarding him?" I ask. "That sounds like something a behaviorist like Skinner might do."
>
> Carl grins at the mention of a theory he's debated against with Skinner himself. "That's okay," he says. "If it works, it works. The important thing is that the employee feels good about it—not manipulated in any way. Then the boss could continue to inquire as to where the employee is at each step, so that both are having input into the process."

"And the boss could be honestly open about what he's doing," I add, raising my eyebrows to make sure we're on the same wavelength.

"Yes," Carl continues in his reassuring manner. "First and foremost, he needs to be honest and candid about what he's trying to accomplish. His open honesty will encourage the employee to take bigger risks, if he feels the boss is on his side."

"So mistakes are okay."

"How else can he learn?" continues Carl. "The successful boss has to really want his employee to grow, and mistakes are part of learning. The employee needs to know that his boss is committed to this learning process. Otherwise, it could break down."

6

The Origins of
Emotional Intelligence

When I do truly hear a person and the meanings that are
important to him at that moment, hearing not simply his
words, but *him*, and when I let him know that I have heard his
own private personal meanings, many things happen. There is
first of all a grateful look. He feels released. He wants to tell me
more about his world. He surges forth in a new sense of
freedom. I think he becomes more open to the process of
change.

—CARL ROGERS, *Freedom to Learn*

The history of the concept of emotional intelligence can be traced
back through many decades to one of the renegades of the psy-
choanalytic school—Otto Rank. Departing from the theoretical
teachings of his mentor, Sigmund Freud, Rank said in a 1938
lecture delivered at the University of Minnesota:

From my own experience, I learned that the therapeutic process is
basically an *emotional experience*—which takes place independently
of the theoretical concepts of the analyst. . . . Simply speaking, this is
the definition of relationship: *one individual is helping the other to*

develop and grow, without infringing too much on the other's personality. (Rank/Kramer, 1938/1996, p. 271)

Among those whom Rank's comments influenced was a young, shy professor of psychology who was to change the face of American psychology, if not its entire communication culture. Carl Ransom Rogers was a renegade like Otto Rank. Challenging the Freudian underpinnings of American psychotherapy in the 1940s, Rogers took the ideas he heard Rank discuss and applied them to solving the problems of GIs returning from World War II. Decades later, in his 1980 book *A Way of Being,* Rogers described the essence of his approach to interpersonal communication:

> It means entering the private perceptual world of the other and becoming thoroughly at home in it. It involves being sensitive, moment to moment, to the changing felt meanings which flow in this other person to the fear or rage or tenderness or confusion or whatever, that he or she is experiencing. It means temporarily living in the other's life, moving about it delicately without making judgments; it means sensing meanings of which he or she is scarcely aware, but not trying to uncover totally unconscious feelings, since this would be too threatening. (p. 142)

According to Rogers, such communication can be accomplished only when one is nonjudgmental about the outcome and feels sufficient inner strength to yield to the other without fear of being engulfed.

Above all, maintained Rogers, is the authentic personality. "I have not found it to be helpful or effective in my relationships with other people to try to maintain a facade; to act in one way on the surface when I am experiencing something quite different underneath," said Rogers in a 1956 presentation in Urbana, Illinois. He went on to say, "Real relationships have an exciting way of being vital and meaningful . . . Real relationships tend to change rather than to remain static . . . So I find it effective to let myself be what I am in my attitudes." With this approach to listening, he could hear the depth of what others were saying much more clearly. And such listening results in deep change, Rogers found.

PIONEERING IN THE CLASSROOM

Rogers discovered that his principles were easier to articulate than to apply, as he read the weekly reaction sheets he invited his students to write. At the end of the first week of class, one student wrote "of uncomfortableness and apprehension." Another wrote: "The class seems to be lacking in planning and direction." Another used the word "disappointing," adding, "I keep wishing the *course* would start," referring to the lack of imposed structure in Rogers' class. And yet one more wrote, "I liked listening, liked hearing the voices . . . but . . . I felt a terrifying distance."

By the fourth week of class, one student wrote of an awareness of "my dislike of the fuzzy, and my liking for the clear-cut." But an indication that the group was turning the corner was reflected in another student's reaction: "The past week proved to be the most fruitful one for the birth and development of new ideas in a long, long time."

A foreign student in the class wrote somewhat awkwardly: "There is no need to say that it takes a long time for people to get rid of their habits regardless of whether or not their habits are sterile, infertile, or barren."

As the weeks went by, student comments became more favorable. For example:

> I've been caught up by the idea that "listening is contagious." . . . I want to express the strong feeling I have this week: I like us all so much. . . . And I think that's where listening comes in. It seems to me as if somehow I have shaken off my rigidity in relating to other people in the class. Now, instead of a categorical response, I can listen, and I hear. (Rogers, 1995, p. 16)

One student who reacted to the class with strong silence and critical, sarcastic weekly reaction sheets had this to say in the final evaluation of the course:

Again and again in my mind these past few days I have found myself thinking about this darn class; I don't seem to be able to escape it. I find myself thinking again and again of a quotation which I cannot remember in its entirety—it's from Walter Whitman, I think, and it goes something like this— "Have you learned lessons only of those who were easy with you . . . have you not learned great lessons from those who disputed the passionate with you?" (1995, p. 17)

Rogers himself summarized his experiment with this challenging, new form of truthful communication, which we currently place in the context of emotional intelligence, as follows:

I have found that when I can permit myself to understand the students in my classes and their real feelings, the whole interactional experience becomes much more valuable for them and for me. For myself, this is an extension of what I have already learned in counseling with individuals, that to understand another person's private world of feelings is a mutually rewarding experience. (1995, p. 18)

PIONEERING THE WORKPLACE

The workplace as we've known it has been characterized by a hierarchy of dominance, in which each individual's function was limited and curtailed by an assignment within the hierarchy. What Rogers advocated was a reassessment of hierarchical rigidity to free up human potential for greater contribution, greater vision and intrinsic motivation to reach for one's best.

The more an individual feels free to be creative and to satisfy his curiosity in solving problems, the more fruitful will be such effort. As we enter an era of growing self-management, Rogers' introduction to what we now know as emotional intelligence allows for "getting people into better communication with one another . . . and helping them get feedback from others" (Evans, 1975, p. 32).

Rogers predicted that hierarchy would yield to self-management when he wrote in 1980: "The more complex the structure—whether a chemical or human—the more energy it expends to maintain that complexity" (1980, p. 131). We now know more clearly that smaller groups can respond to shifting customer needs much more rapidly and effectively than a rigid hierarchy.

In his own work across the country, Rogers and his associates predated what we now refer to as self-managed teams. "We are a thoroughly open staff, with no leaders and no hierarchical organization. Leadership and responsibility are shared. We have become a very close team . . ." (1980, p. 188).

PIONEERING IN WORLD POLITICS

In his later years, Rogers turned his attention increasingly to world politics and attempted to do what he could to defuse such international hot spots as Ireland and South America. He compared the "old guard" politics with the new. Old guard politics he characterized as hierarchically based, with little trust and a constant state of fear. Instead, he advocated that responsibility be shared on the basis of trusting that individuals can think for themselves. Projects could be developed through open communication rather than behind closed doors. Discipline could come from within rather than by external threat. All this could result not only in higher morale but in greater productivity.

Rogers worked with an initially hostile group from Belfast, Northern Ireland, made up of both Protestants and Catholics, including extremists on both sides. Despite centuries-old bitterness between the two groups, Rogers was able to achieve a level of communication that transformed each individual. The meetings were filmed and the result was shown by teams—one Protestant and one Catholic—to many groups.

CARTER'S CAMP DAVID EXPERIMENT

Rogers then turned his attention to another historic enmity—that between Arabs and Israelis. He and I analyzed the success of President Carter's meeting with Israeli Prime Minister Menachem Begin and Egyptian President Anwar Sadat at Camp David in 1978, resulting in a peace accord that still stands (Rogers and Ryback, 1984).

Rogers and I concluded that the success of this highly revolutionary form of international negotiation came about because of the informality of the meetings and—unheard of until this time—having no set agenda, except for the overriding aim of achieving peace. The steps toward the goal were not set up in advance, nor was the scheduling of meetings—in other words, no rules and no preconditions. Emotional expression was encouraged; even shouting matches were permitted.

With such emotional dynamics, of course, there were ups and downs. At one point, as frustration followed frustration, Moshe Dayan felt that a "mood of anger gave way to sadness and disappointment" (Dayan, 1981, p. 174).

At another point, Carter's attempts at refereeing seemed to flounder. "All restraint was now gone. Their faces were flushed, and the niceties of diplomatic language and protocol were stripped away . . . Begin had touched a raw nerve, and I thought Sadat would explode. He pounded the table . . ." (Carter, 1982, p. 351).

Clearly, the negotiators felt the searing intensity of open feelings about deeply held cultural differences. Feelings of disappointment and failure were overcome by poignant intimate meetings in which Carter discussed Begin's grandchildren, for example, to persuade him not to give up. He offered photographs of himself personally inscribed to each of Begin's grandchildren.

As Carter handed Begin the photos, "His lips trembled and tears welled up in his eyes. . . . We were both emotional as we talked quietly for a few minutes about grandchildren and about war" (Carter, 1982, p. 399). This brought about a dramatic shift in Begin's attitude. Taking the bit in his teeth, he marched over to Sadat's cabin, unaccompanied by any of his staff. No one else knows exactly what happened there. Carter, concerned that the two chiefs of state might need a mediator to cool things off, made his way there as soon as he could, only to find a satisfied Begin leaving Sadat's cabin. "He was quite happy," wrote Carter, "as he told me they had had a love feast and that Sadat had agreed to Begin's language on the Knesset vote" (Carter, 1982, p. 400). These early applications of emotional intelligence to international negotiations mark an important milestone. Although emotions ran rampant at times, President Carter as facilitator was an excellent model of emotional intelligence, for the following reasons.

1. He was self-motivated in setting up the Camp David meetings, risking his own reputation as well as the prestige of his office.

2. He was keenly aware of the emotional dynamics of all parties, responding to Begin's resignation to failure by reaching out with sympathy and generosity, for example.

3. He managed outbreaks of anger between the introverted Sadat and the extroverted Begin. "There was no compatibility between the two men," wrote Carter, "and almost every discussion of any subject deteriorated into an unproductive argument, reopening the old wounds of past political or military battles" (Carter, 1982, p. 355). Emotional intelligence allows for the expression of emotion. The key is in handling it and making it productive, which Carter ultimately succeeded in doing.

4. Superior management skill is the keystone of executive intelligence, and Carter proved effective here by meeting with individuals on a one-to-one basis when that was called for, making himself open and intimate at such times.

5. He injected a touch of humor at other times when tension became particularly palpable. For example, after a particularly long and heavy silence, Carter "tried to break the tension by telling Begin that if he would sign the document as written, it would save us all a lot of time . . . everyone broke into gales of genuine laughter" (Carter, 1982, p. 345).

When shouting echoed between the opposing parties, Carter stood strong and either interfered with a plea for increased mutual trust or sat back and took notes. When the shouting finally ended, he would read from his notes about the real issues dividing the countries and transform the hostile mood into one of thoughtful recognition of the deeper issues. With this emotionally intelligent approach, Carter effectively controlled outbursts of anger, promoted hope when defeat seemed imminent and, ultimately, produced harmony out of chaos.

In the history of the use of emotional intelligence, Carter's Camp David efforts are exemplary. According to *New Yorker's* Richard Rovere (1978), "Carter's plans for Camp David violated all the rules of modern summitry. The first of these is that heads of state and government do not come together until they have been assured by ambassadors and other negotiators that firm, enforceable agreements have been concluded and wait only their seals and signatures" (p. 135).

As pioneer of the emotionally intelligent approach to international politics, President Carter demonstrated how a genuinely sincere, emotionally perceptive, nonjudgmental attitude can help bitter opponents understand one another sufficiently to bridge centuries-old enmity. By supporting the truth and smoothing out opposing versions of it, by offering support when hope flagged and by resolving conflict in a challenging manner with both zeal and self-assurance, Carter was able to encourage two enemies to greater levels of risk-taking in pursuit of achieving peace. That the Camp David meetings succeeded when nothing else since Biblical times had, is a bright page in the history of the application of emotional intelligence.

CONCLUSION

The skills demonstrated by President Carter will be described in greater depth in Chapter 9. For now, however, let's move on to see how Carter's Camp David innovations can fit into your office, and exactly what make up the elements of executive intelligence.

Can Carl Rogers' experiment in truth and President Carter's experiment in conflict resolution be useful for self-managed teams in today's workplace? Absolutely! Mutual trust and confidence can take the place of frustration and resentment. Team pride can be fostered by mutual appreciation and synergistic effort. Although critics fear that this may create a sense of dependency, a commitment to ongoing constructive "conflict"— candid, honest feedback based on mutual respect and support— can make for a productive interdependency instead.

In the next chapter, we'll contrast the old and new leadership styles and look at a couple of studies illustrating that social skills may be much more important to successful leadership than personality or IQ.

7

How Executive Intelligence Works

Fearless minds climb soonest unto crowns.

—SHAKESPEARE, *Henry VI*

NOT IQ OR PERSONALITY BUT SOCIAL SKILLS

You may consider that emotional needs have no place in business meetings. Certainly, the New Team Ethic can be abused by a few very needy individuals who are not above abusing any system. That's a danger to guard against, of course. Even the best cars or airplanes can be easily destroyed by destructive drivers or pilots. Aside from such abuse, the New Team Ethic can prove extremely effective. Like any new system or technology, it takes some training for most effective results. That will be offered later in this book. The important thing for now is to decide whether or not the New Team Ethic is for you.

In order to help you decide allow me to share a study reported in a 1993 edition of the *Harvard Business Review*. Robert Kelley and Janet Caplan studied a division of Bell Labs responsible for designing and creating electronic telephone switches. This division is made up of teams ranging in size from 5 to 150. Their work is very challenging and demanding and their results quite successful. Kelley and Caplan asked these hardworking scientists and engineers to nominate the top 10 to 15 percent who stood out as stars.

When compared with their less stellar co-workers, these industrial-strength superstars were found to differ very little from the others, scoring very similarly on tests of IQ and personality, as well as on college grades. Kelley and Caplan were stymied. They were determined to ferret out the difference, so they interviewed their subjects in greater depth.

What they discovered was startling. What made the difference between the stars and the others was their ability to establish rapport with key people in the larger network within the division, people who had the technical answers and who offered them freely and quickly because of the rapport built over time. The star could now return to her group with the needed answer and avoid any further delay on the group's now quick road to achieving its goal. "Social intelligence," as pioneering psychologist E. L. Thorndike referred to it, made all the difference, not IQ or any other personality quality.

Imagine yourself a member of a working team. Your goal is to design and implement an ad campaign for a product that has just a slight edge over the competition. The product will fail unless the consumer can learn to appreciate that marginal difference through the success of your ad campaign. If this isn't a common scenario, I don't know what is!

THE OLD AND THE NEW

Now, you can choose to be on one of two teams. The members of both teams are equally intelligent and talented in their respective specialties. In fact, the membership of both teams is identical except for, you guessed it, their *emotional intelligence*.

Old Team sits stoically, with little expression on its members' faces, a few of them smoking nervously. Their talk sounds serious and important, but it soon becomes apparent that many of the imperious-sounding statements are largely repetitious and uninspiring. A few yawns give evidence that no one dares to challenge the status quo. Pretty soon the activity is limited to two or three members who are reduced to arguing some petty aspects of the larger problem. Eventually, people start surreptitiously glancing at their watches as their body language signifies they're already absent from the present meeting and anticipating their next activity.

New Team members, on the other hand, sit excitedly at the edges of their chairs. The discussion is dynamic as one excited participant after another enters into the verbal fray, punctuated by occasional laughter. There is a bright, healthy look on their faces.

The conversation, as I've mentioned, is full of excitement. Participants talk not only on the scheduled topic, but of their own feelings and opinions as well. There is a sense of mutual caring of each for all the other group members. No one is left out. Even the shyest member is given a fair share of sincere attention. When a long-winded member goes on too long, a friendly comment indicates it's time to hear someone who hasn't yet spoken. One member takes it upon himself to take notes on the many new ideas issuing forth. Another member announces she wishes to attempt to consolidate the more productive suggestions. When time for the meeting finally runs out, some shake hands warmly, congratulating one another on their inspiring contributions. A few others linger, expressing appreciation on learning a new facet of their co-worker's life experience.

Which team would you rather be on? More important, which team do you suppose will have the more productive discussion? As I'm sure you've guessed, the New Team employs the New Team Ethic of executive intelligence. Old Team has just been let go, "victim" of downsizing.

THE NEW LEADERSHIP

Sure, I'm stacking the deck by oversimplifying and exaggerating, but only to make a point. Even following the New Team Ethic of encouraging balance between emotion and logic, any new self-managed group will face challenges, especially at the beginning. The first challenge of any new group is to ferret out the conflict for dominance. Until this is openly dealt with, no group can reach its potential of executive intelligence. There is no simple formula for resolving this conflict, innate in virtually every beginning group.

Old Team would most likely rely on the organizational chart for its awareness of dominance hierarchy. Whoever had the highest rank would be deferred to the most. For New Team, it's not so simple. The organizational chart is soon ignored as the ideas of those most knowledgeable, sincere and confident begin to garner the most respect. This newfound respect will either be enhanced or destroyed, depending on how fair-mindedly this member shares the group attention she earned with those less confident, yet with worthwhile and sincere contributions. The group will have a sense of trust that will ensure this new leader's respect if she uses the newly acquired role fairly and wisely.

In addition, the priorities of the discussion may change and another leader may emerge with an expertise relating to the newly emerged topic. It's as if a "situational leadership" of expertise has been recognized. Leadership may shift dynamically in New Team, and since it emerges from an organic and informal group consent, the shift is smooth and agreeable.

What makes all this possible is the emotional honesty, or emotional intelligence, of the group members. New Team's underlying agenda is not control or power as it often is in conventional groups, but a clear focus on productive problem solving. Personal needs for attention and social status or acceptance are met directly and forthrightly by ensuring the right of each member to be heard as long as the comment is sincere, independent of the value of its contribution. Somehow, this sincere attention brings out the best in people's thinking. And since each member is rewarded by group attention for sincerity, real needs for attention and support are directly met.

Time magazine writer Walter Isaacson attended one of Bill Gates' Microsoft meetings, and wrote, "Gates doesn't address anyone by name, hand out praise or stroke any egos. But he listens intently, democratically. . . . No one seems to be showing off or competing for attention, but neither do any hesitate to speak up or challenge Gates" (1997, p. 54).

BRING OUT THE TOYS

An excellent model for managing with executive intelligence is the late Wernher von Braun, the early chief of NASA. Von Braun was certainly a technical genius, but in that respect he probably differed very little from his 124 compatriots lured to America from Nazi Germany under the guise of Operation Paper Clip. What made von Braun stand out and helped him lead NASA through years of successful pioneering space flight was his undeniable genius for understanding, engaging and motivating those under him as well as the congressmen and senators from whom he had to obtain funding for NASA activities. I can think of no better model for combining the best of intellect and emotional awareness in order to bring out the best in others. When von Braun had to make presentations to government committees, he engaged his audiences' emotions with model rockets. "You know how to handle these senators and congressmen?" he once shared with a friend. "You get down on the floor with them and bring out the models and toys—graphics, if necessary—and you show them. Thus you get the money. It works every time. Look at my track record. I've never been turned down" (Adair, 1996).

Sure, von Braun had the technical and engineering expertise, but just as important, he understood the emotions of congressmen and senators, many of whom came from simple, agricultural backgrounds. He knew how to get to them. He had emotional intelligence, and used it wisely.

In the same issue of the *Harvard Business Review* as the Kelley-Caplan study, David Krackhardt and Jeffrey R. Hanson (1993) describe three informal networks that operate behind the scenes: communication webs of a social nature; expertise networks for technical advice; and trust networks whose people may share some of their more private and less socially acceptable feelings.

The stars described by Kelley and Caplan were popular in the informal networks as well as in the more obvious formal networks. Their emotional intelligence involved the following six skills:

1. The ability to see things from others' perspectives.

2. Persuasiveness.

3. The ability to form consensus out of apparent chaos.

4. The knack of avoiding conflict.

5. The ability to coordinate the efforts of others, resulting in effective teamwork.

6. The desire to go beyond their job descriptions and the ability to structure their time in order to accomplish these additional self-chosen tasks.

CONCLUSION

Workplace superstars, like the ones studied by Kelley and Caplan, set an energetic pace that helps give the group a sense of purposeful identity. With such a clear focus on goal attainment, a sense of team pride develops with each step toward success. Top-level management can contribute to this by recognizing such efforts. The net result promotes the New Team Ethic—success through self-managed team effort, characterized by emotionally open communication, support and recognition of each other's natural skills, and the self-discipline motivated by the challenge to grow into one's own natural abilities and emerging talents. In this chapter I described how self-managing teams can use emotional openness to solidify team purpose and motivation.

Now that you know how emotional intelligence works, that a large part of it is the ability to establish rapport within a group and with informally related groups as well, in Chapter 8 you'll have the opportunity to explore the basic assumptions and values that underlie the framework of emotional intelligence and self-management. We'll begin by comparing the values of self-management with those of conventional management.

8

The Assumptions of Self-Management

I never heard
So musical a discord, such sweet thunder.

—SHAKESPEARE, *Midsummer Night's Dream*

Although consensus is the hallmark of self-management, consensus without any disagreement coming into play may be a sign of danger. It may indicate that the consensus is false if it has not been achieved through some discussion of opposing opinion. There is always the danger of "consensus by identification"— saying "yes" because that's what the boss thinks. Discussion is the medium of consensus; consensus without discussion is false consensus.

The emotionally intelligent CEO is at the same time a facilitator of honest communication and the bearer of ultimate responsibility. He or she must be sensitive to the dynamics of the moment as well as the distant horizon; sensitive to input, yet independent in making ultimate decisions; emotionally aware, yet well organized with information; forgiving of weakness, yet rewarding of strength.

If this sounds like conventional leadership, think again. There is a clear distinction between conventional and emotionally intelligent business leadership. Here are some of the distinctions.

Conventional Management	Self-Management
Structured as hierarchy according to organizational thought	Structure is informal, based on flow of communication through group process
Policies relate to general principles	Problems are resolved according to particular situation
Personnel policies are applied to all indifferently	Personnel policies can apply to each person uniquely
Emotional considerations are disparaged	Emotional considerations are encouraged
Individual achievement is encouraged	Group enterprise is encouraged
Distinctions are marked between boss and employee	Each individual is empowered to rise to level of potential
Customers are seen as "on the other side of the counter"	Customers are seen as partners

If I had to distill the most important difference between conventional and self-management, I'd characterize conventional management as focused on goal-oriented achievement, and self-management as providing empowerment through relevant contribution. The difference lies in valuing the individual at least as much as goal achievement. Although both systems respect individual dignity, integrity in relationships and social responsibility, the self-management approach has a stronger emphasis on these virtues.

The appreciation of the individual's contribution to self-managexment leads to a new awareness of the extrinsic value of this human factor, which is becoming known as "human capital," a value now to be added to structural capital (see Malone, 1997). As communications technology continues to change at an accelerating rate, human capital becomes more and more critical. Those whose job it is to keep pace with such changes are an increasingly precious commodity.

Human capital and structural capital make up the totality of intellectual capital. Specifically, human capital refers to the knowledge, skills and overall experience of individuals, while structural capital refers to the "software" belonging to humans—organizational concepts, information about customers and suppliers, expertise in technologies, and so on.

An emotionally intelligent enterprise assigns a high value to its intellectual assets and takes steps to retain such assets. The collective knowledge it can accumulate and retain is just as valuable as its nonhuman and noninformation assets. It will not be long before accounting procedures actually measure such intellectual assets along with buildings, equipment and cash reserves.

GUIDELINES FOR MAXIMIZING THE USE OF INTELLECTUAL CAPITAL IN THE WORKPLACE

Intellectual capital is made up of business smarts that make the difference. Software that simulates human intelligence in decision making complements human wisdom in coming up with the best ultimate solution. Push technology makes electronic information highly accessible, when relevant data are needed quickly. All the data are available. But ultimately the human mind must sift through them and take final responsibility.

Data, after all, are only numbers, derived from combinations of one and zero. They have no meaning in and of themselves other than what we attribute to them. Data can be accurate or inaccurate but not right or wrong in terms of value.

Bits and data are to information what molecules and cells are to the organism. Just as individuals have unique personalities, so does information since it takes on a life of its own, but only as we humans interact with it. Without the human touch, data are like the sounds of a tree falling in an empty forest. With no one to hear it, does the sound exist other than as mere waves of compressed air?

So how does the New Team Ethic approach the electronic age of information? By giving priority to the free flow of information from the human component of the corporate knowledge base. How can that be done? By maximizing quality output in a mutually supportive, relevancy-based arena of open discussion. Here's how to encourage the best use of intellectual capital in an environment overflowing with electronic data.

- All individuals involved in the research and development, manufacture, production, sales and marketing aspects of a company can be sources of innovative and profitable suggestions.
- The most emotionally intelligent perspective for all these individuals is that of the consumer.
- Each department head can have an emotionally intelligent awareness of the needs of all other departments within the division, as can each division head of all other divisions. This awareness can come about through any number of communication processes—group meetings, e-mail, newsletters.
- Quality is a priority in which all can take both individual and collective pride. It is the point of relevance that becomes the criterion for appreciating individual contributions. Suggestions are valued to the extent they contribute to quality.
- Executives become facilitators for their staff members in the process of creative innovation and enhancement of quality. Communication is not one way from the top down. It even goes beyond two-way communication: It becomes a dy-

namic process of open discussion where innovation and quality emerge from the relatively unstructured process in the self-management groups.

- Discipline emerges from commitment to innovation and quality in terms of individual accountability. Say what you want when you want, so long as it's on target and respectful of others' relevant contributions.
- Any individual who upsets the efficient flow of team discussion through seeking attention, at the cost of productive communication, will be held accountable. Although such individuals can be given the "benefit of the doubt" for a while, if there is an indisputable consensus of group frustration with the individual that persists, then action must be taken, privately at first or collectively if that doesn't work.

THE EVOLUTION OF SELF-MANAGEMENT IN JAPAN

Open communication can cut through the skepticism and cynicism that often stand in the way of progress. Look at what such communication has done for Japanese industry!

The Japanese, after World War II, became adept at copying and running off tremendous numbers of Western-style products at relatively little expense and shipping them off to the United States. With cheap labor and authoritarian management, they could forge ahead and beat the United States at the game of mass production.

As the decades went by, though, the Japanese began to copy Western techniques of management instead. Whatever Americans were discussing in books and seminars, the valiant Japanese began to practice and to improve! As time went by, authoritarian management shifted inexorably to a type of enlightened feudalism in which each corporation become a family of support for its employees in return for unquestioned and durable loyalty.

Within each corporation and within the component divisions, responsibility and accountability were shared, down to the basic levels of enterprise. Americans knew of this approach by such terms as "Theory Z" and "Total Quality." The Japanese have their own term for this style of management—*kaizen.*

The two primary characteristics of *kaizen* are:

- Products can be improved on a continual basis.
- Each individual in the process of manufacture and development has the opportunity to contribute innovative ideas and suggestions.

The second point is very close to the basic assumption of self-management in the framework of the new executive intelligence. Each person has the right to be heard, and contributions are measured on the basis of sincerity and relevance.

The effect of this emotionally intelligent use of intellectual capital is staggering. There is no greater inspiration to creative productivity than being challenged to one's full potential. Consider the opposite, where individuals are put to mind-numbing routine tasks despite their ability to provide much more. There is nothing more devastating to the inner spirit.

By offering each individual the opportunity to contribute to the best of his or her ability, the Japanese have been in the forefront of innovative technology and now increasingly in the area of financial management. The Japanese have outpaced their American counterparts with their emotionally intelligent perspective of identifying the needs of the consumer more quickly.

CONCLUSION

As corporate America enters the twenty-first century, an emotionally intelligent approach in the workplace can enhance the innovative capacities of its workforce, raising the collective self-esteem of American industry. As well, the members of each self-managed team can enjoy a greater degree of self-respect for individual contribution.

Ayn Rand (1957) wrote, "The quickest way to kill the human spirit is to ask someone to do mediocre work." I would add, the quickest way to lift the human spirit is to ask someone to offer their best. Mihaly Csikszentmihaly (1990) writes of the serene flow of optimal experience, where one is doing one's most creative, productive work and enjoying the sublime experience to such an extent that time seems to disappear. At such times we are filled with grace, and the results of our efforts are of the highest value. By allowing each individual to contribute to his or her most creative potential, the highest value of the workforce— in terms of bottom-line profits—is attained. This is not only about feel-good experience; it's also about net profit dollars.

Not only does an emotionally intelligent approach to self-management promote productivity and increase profits, it also offers personal benefits in terms of enhanced self-awareness, control over stress-inducing emotions, more effective self-motivation and superior management skills. In the next chapter we'll explore how these personal benefits can be taught.

Can an organization learn emotional intelligence? How long does it take? What are the components of such a program? These are the questions that are answered in the following chapter.

Part III
Emotionally Intelligent Leadership

"What about training?" I ask out of the blue. "I mean, is there a way the boss could train his employee so that, first of all, it's accomplished more effectively and, second, it's more meaningful and interesting for both?"

"I'm sure there is," Carl responds instantly, but then reflects for a while. "For example, asking open-ended questions might be an excellent way to get the employee thinking in the right direction. That'd be much better than just giving him directions and instructions."

"Encouraging him in a more creative direction," I add.

"Yes," continues Carl. "The more the employee feels . . . a sense of involvement . . ."

"A sense of control, too?"

"That too, I guess. The main point is that the employee feel that he's contributing from his own sense of values, his own frame of reference . . ."

"So that he can identify with his contribution," I add, "to call it his own?"

"Making him more of an equal partner," continues Carl, "not coming from a one-down position."

"I guess the boss may have something to learn, too," I surmise. "I mean, he's still a human being, after all, and the employee can know that—"

"It's a matter of trust," interrupts Carl. "Does the boss trust his employee to use his own resources—"

"And then the employee, in turn, can trust his boss. If the boss begins with trust, then his employee can trust back."

"And be much more open to learning and growth," adds Carl, "so he can be a more effective worker. After all, a person's work is a big part of his life."

"Sure is," I agree. "He spends more time there than in any other single place. I never thought of it like that. It's as important as his family, at least in terms of hours spent."

"It's a major reflection of one's life. Bosses don't usually think of their employees that way. To many, the worker is just someone to fill a niche or complete a task. To the worker, it's a major part of his life."

"So respect and having a sense of value is important to his self-esteem as an employee," I add. "Even the word 'employee' has somewhat of a dehumanizing tone to it."

"Yes." Carl has an edge of excitement to his voice again. "If they can both be more fully human, not confined to their roles as boss and employee, then I'm darn sure they'd be more effective at what they do."

"What's that term you use in your writing?" I ask. "You know . . . congruence. Yes, that's it. If they can both be congruent or honest—authentic—about their feelings . . ."

"It isn't easy," says Carl. "I sometimes catch myself, or someone close to me might remind me, that I'm totally oblivious to some feeling or other that rightfully deserves my attention."

"You mean you're human, Carl?"

" 'Fraid so," he chuckles. "How 'bout we start walking back? This is farther than I usually walk, but I don't want to overdo it."

"So how do boss and employee get rid of the conventional . . . boundaries or restriction, and become more of a team of open, honest workers, so they can function at a more efficient level, more open to their potential?" I ask, as we turn back in the opposite direction. "Without defining roles, isn't there a danger of confusion, of too much emotional openness, getting in the way of the work at hand?"

"Well, I've thought about that, David. I don't think the roles are given up completely. But within his role, the boss can still let his employee know that he'd like to be a better boss by getting feedback about how to do so. He can't get better as a boss unless he gets this feedback."

"So boss stays boss and employee stays employee," I say, "but within those roles, they can be more honest about the interaction between them. In other words, employees are people too, not necessarily inferior to the boss, and they appreciate the respect of an emotionally honest boss."

"Yes," says Carl. "The point is to get the job accomplished to the best of the ability of both. The employee can do a much better job—"

"If he's respected for his viewpoint, his perspective," I interrupt.

"Yes, if his deeper perspective is taken into account, not just his limited job description."

"So they contribute equally in a way, but the boss still assumes the bulk of the responsibility."

"Yes," says Carl. "That's his charge, and he can never give that up."

"Unless he does so formally and publicly, unless, in other words, he promotes the individual and changes his place in the hierarchy. So there still is a place for hierarchy and organizational charts."

"I guess so," concedes Carl, "unless there's a decision to work in teams—"

"You mean, without hierarchy?"

"Without," confirms Carl. "That way they could concentrate fully on the task at hand without worrying about things like chain of command. Everyone would be equally responsible or accountable, so you'd have the best of both worlds—responsible, hard-working employees and bosses getting their hands dirty without worrying about the limitations of roles. Of course, it would have to be done right. I guess it could backfire too."

"What do you mean, Carl?"

"They'd have to be real sure about their goals and agree on how to achieve them. They'd have to be real close as a group, to be able to read one another quite clearly. Most important, they'd have to be able to handle conflict in the group openly and not sweep it under the rug."

"But wouldn't that take away from the group cohesiveness?"

"No," answers Carl. "As a matter of fact, I've found that the best groups, maybe all groups that survive as an effective team, typically have inner conflict among the members, particularly at the beginning. If the conflict is kept from coming to the surface, then that group or team will never function at its highest potential. But, once they deal with that conflict, and resolve it among themselves, then I'd be happy to be a member of such a team."

"What's the conflict usually about?"

"I'm not quite sure." Carl hesitates and looks off in the direction of the sun lowering toward the horizon. "Control, maybe, or some kind of informal leadership hierarchy."

"So perhaps there's a . . . replacement, another kind of internal structure."

"I wouldn't be surprised," reflects Carl. "But this new, informal hierarchy is much more finely tuned to the true, deeper characteristics of each of the team members."

"So each of the individuals feels more comfortable now."

"Yes, just like a custom-tailored shoe fits much more comfortably than one bought off the shelf."

9

Learning Emotional Intelligence

A little learning is a dangerous thing:
Drink deep, or taste not the Pierian spring.

—POPE, *Essay on Criticism*

Many, if not most, executives in today's workplace have much to learn about emotional intelligence. For better or worse, a keen sense of competition and ambition is more characteristic of those who climb the hierarchical ladder than the laid-back sensitivity of those who may lag behind. Being emotionally intelligent is neither about being competitive nor about being laid back. It's about using your emotional sensitivity, whatever your level of intensity. In the process of climbing the corporate ladder, many have little time or energy to learn the skills and benefits of emotional intelligence. Those who do ascend the corporate ladder without it will do even better once they acquire it.

For people at all levels on the organizational chart, stress in the workplace is a continuing problem. As the workplace becomes more competitive and demanding, executive intelligence becomes more important, not only for reduction of stress and absenteeism, but also for more effective, productive management.

The demand for management training continues to grow in response to these needs. Most such training, however, does not address the core of effective communication that is the focus of training on executive intelligence. Therefore such training is highly personal and carries over into personal life skills as well.

At times training in emotional intelligence involves a change in basic personal values, and may even pose a threat to those with rigid value systems. Certainly, such training impacts on social style, possibly affecting (no doubt improving) the communication of emotions within the family setting. This type of training goes very deep, and is very personal.

Emotional intelligence is not targeted to any particular group—it can be used by all who desire more effective and productive management. If it also turns out to improve social skills outside the workplace and personal relations at home, all the better. A happier person at home will more likely make a more productive employee at work.

Since executive intelligence training hits so deeply, it can hardly be learned overnight, or even over a five-day program, though that's definitely a good beginning. Such training goes on indefinitely, with periodic refresher courses and ongoing weekly or monthly reminder sessions. Let's take a look at one such program instituted in Japan.

A TRAINING PROGRAM—MADE IN JAPAN

Akiri Ikemi of Okayama University and Shinya Kubota of the University of Occupational and Environmental Health in Japan structured a five-day training program in emotional intelligence as follows (Ikemi and Kubota, 1996):

Day 1: Basic theory of mental health concepts, stress management and relaxation training, active listening exercises,
followed by videotaping of these skills and, as a reward for
the first day's work, an evening party.

Day 2: Theory, feedback on 3-minute video segments of all
participants, more active listening training, sharing and
questions.

Day 3: Active listening in triads, training for focusing
on feeling, training for listening for feeling, followed by
video recordings of participants' efforts to use their new
skills.

Day 4: Learning to focus on inner emotions, active listening of
felt emotion in others, sharing and questions.

Day 5: Less structured than the other four days. Participants
can share what they've learned, how they feel about it,
the challenges of implementation and anything else that
comes up.

Ikemi and Kubota developed this structure while working with
an automobile manufacturer, two chemical corporations, two
steel corporations and a manufacturer of medical supplies. The
participants were managers and administrators, and were tested
before and after the training to ensure that they had indeed
learned the skills they were being taught.

In an earlier chapter, I described the benefits of executive
intelligence in terms of reduction of stress, depression and
anxiety at work. In addition, Ikemi and Kubota found that one
of their individual participants found himself "amazed at the
unique solutions workers came up with" once they became
comfortable with the application of emotional intelligence. "He
also found that, in this way of sharing the decision-making process, workers developed a sense of autonomy and unity among
themselves." His workers reported that "stormy interactions had
diminished, and, in general, they found the manager to be a
'nicer' person" (Ikemi and Kubota, 1996, p. 116).

ADDITIONAL EXERCISES

In addition to such five-day programs, there are specific exercises that can be helpful in one-day or half-day training sessions. One exercise that I've developed involves breaking the larger group down into smaller groups of five to eight people. The small groups are invited to focus on any problem that any of its members wants to bring up as a real-life challenge to be solved. The groups work on their respective solutions for a while and are then asked to reflect among themselves on how much and which aspects of emotional intelligence were employed. They are then asked to switch roles and coach one another on improving their use of emotional intelligence. That is, if one member thinks another has done well, she can now reenact those skills, to be coached by the first member. Similarly, if one of the members considers another to be lacking in skills, the more "emotionally intelligent" member can coach the other. In this sharing process, all can learn and benefit from one another, free of external structure. It should be noted that this exercise can be used independently of the basic five-day program. It allows for each group to learn and teach exactly those component skills needed for particular individuals in each group. Also, it provides a somewhat realistic situation, with minimal external structure, best for learning the skills of emotional intelligence.

Another exercise, which I call "Name that Feeling," invites each group to come up with a recent, real-life, on-the-job conflict. Roles are assigned to simulate the situation and the conflict is reenacted. Then the players are invited to name the hurt or vulnerability behind the conflict. When consensus is finally reached, the players are invited to reenact the conflict, only this time acknowledging the underlying feelings accompanying the anger of their assigned character and asking forthrightly for what they need at a deeper level, which usually has more to do with being understood or appreciated than with the previously stated demands.

Another exercise, one that's been used for years in other contexts, involves each group member advocating the justification for his or her own survival on a boat that needs to get rid of one of its passengers to stay afloat. The only rule is that no one can abdicate. This provides an opportunity for realistic appraisal of self-esteem. "What's so special about me that I should stay aboard?" is the question at hand. The give-and-take of the group members provides for some very thoughtful consideration of positive and negative self-images. The more realistic a positive self-image each member develops, the more facile he will be in employing emotional intelligence.

For another exercise, I sometimes hand out a number of descriptions of somewhat complex scenarios involving two to four individuals to each group, and invite each group to resolve their situations. Then I invite each group to share the essence of their discussions with the larger group. This makes for very lively discussion on the parameters of executive intelligence.

WORKING TOGETHER

One of the issues that each working group must deal with is that of competition for dominance. If the formal hierarchy is put aside for less structured, more natural forms of leadership, then the initial issue is to deal with the natural testing of dominance. Rarely will one individual dominate at first. Some jockeying for position is almost inevitable. But when this is done with honesty and openness, then the natural flow of leadership can emerge quite comfortably. The small training groups can engage in this simulated "jockeying for position" and then provide feedback to one another. This feedback is invaluable to anyone learning a new skill. We can all benefit from an outsider's feedback on our own personal coping style.

Along with honest feedback, the participants offer one another mutual support. Participants are encouraged to articulate what they like about one another in order to become familiar with the concepts of nonjudgmental acceptance of others and appreciation of others as humans, even when conceptual or value differences exist.

This mutual support is essential at a time when participants are learning more about themselves than at any other point in their lives, and this support seems to develop naturally in response to openness with diminished defenses. This is one of the reasons group affinity grows so strongly and quickly, both in real work settings as well as in the training groups.

For this reason, it's preferable to work with participants who work together as well as train together. The group affinity will transfer to the work setting much more easily when the training groups work together as well. It is important that senior officers also take part in the training. If the top layers of management are not part of the shift to the utilization of executive intelligence, then it is bound to fail over time. The core values of a company filter down from the top. The shift to executive intelligence in the workplace is a dramatic one and needs wholehearted support from the top down.

TRAINING FOR IMPULSE CONTROL

The component of emotional intelligence characterized as delayed gratification or impulse control is difficult to teach directly. It's one that grows over time as personality evolves and as character is built. However, it does seem to be an offshoot of learning the other aspects of emotional intelligence.

As individuals feel accepted by the group for their inner emotional being, and as authenticity and emotional honesty become habitual, then the priority of needs seems to shift from the concern of fulfilling solely their own needs to concern for the needs and well-being of the group. It becomes more important for such individuals to be part of the group, to share their values and to integrate their needs with other group members. They are no longer as interested in individual attention or in slighting others to satisfy their own needs. One way of putting it is that as people learn the components of emotional intelligence, they gain character and integrity as well, and delayed gratification or impulse control come along with that.

Of course, controlling the impulse of anger is in a category by itself and is dealt with by variations of the "counting to ten" technique. Indeed, aspects of counting to ten can be used as the first device to control the expression of any emotional impulse, but that option is somewhat simplistic for more socially complex impulses. In any case, regardless of the complexity of the impulse, the habit of "think before you act" is a good starting point.

Conflict resolution exercises, which involve some degree of impulse control, invite group members to analyze conflict-ridden scenarios described in handout sheets. Group members assign themselves to individual characters in the scenario, and explain that vantage point to their group members. Then they switch characters and repeat the process. Shifting from character to character gives them the flexibility to understand others' points of view when they find themselves in conflict situations. In order to lock in these learning experiences, it is suggested that the training participants invite their spouses or companions to acquire at least a rudimentary understanding of the concept of emotional intelligence. What is learned by the couple can strengthen the learning that applies to the workplace. The more comprehensively the new learning can be applied, both at work and at home, the more available it will be at those crucial times when emotions are high and old habits compete with new learning.

Although teaching the new executive intelligence in the workplace is complex and challenging, it is important that those offering such training be carefully selected. It would be wise to employ professionals who are experienced in the process of interpersonal dynamics—trained psychologists or those working closely with them.

BENEFITS OF TRAINING

The benefits of going through training on executive intelligence are many, but ultimately must be reflected in a positive effect on the bottom line, and an increase in overall productivity. Smooth working relations, higher morale, less absenteeism, less turnover, more effective communication, more creative ideas and implementations are all direct results, and these in turn create a superior and more productive and successful workplace where the ultimate criterion, measured in dollars and cents, is easily achieved.

The benefits of training go beyond the workplace. They include better relationships at home and in the rest of one's personal life, better health and a more fulfilling approach to life in general. More specifically, let's take a look at how each of the four components of emotional intelligence can benefit an individual's personal as well as working life.

1. Sharpening your instincts
   - Deeper understanding of one's own feelings and how they affect others
   - More effective process for making personal decisions
   - Increased sensitivity to intercultural differences
2. Controlling your negative emotions
   - Control of anger arising out of conflict at home
   - More effective child-rearing
   - Less marital discord
   - Even getting along with the in-laws
   - Less anxiety and depression in personal life
   - Improved self-image and self-confidence
   - Longer, healthier life span
3. Discovering your talents
   - More compassionate approach to personal relationships
   - Greater likelihood of initiating and following through on continuing education and self-improvement programs
   - Successful completion of personal projects

4. Superior management skills
    - Ability to mediate conflicts within the family
    - Improved communication skills
    - More appreciation by friends for sense of fairness
    - Decrease in ethical transgressions

Not to be overlooked is the likelihood of increased income and promotion for those who integrate the basics of executive intelligence into their work setting. Obviously, this could be expected to enhance the quality of life on a personal level as well.

In the next chapter, we'll take a look at how executives integrate the characteristics of executive intelligence into their leadership styles.

10

The Ten Attributes of Executive Intelligence

Lives of great men all remind us
We can make our lives sublime,
And, departing, leave behind us
Footprints on the sands of time.

—LONGFELLOW, *A Psalm of Life*

How do you become an emotionally intelligent executive? In theory, it's merely a matter of learning the ten personality attributes associated with executive intelligence. In practice, it's more like trying to answer the question "How do you become a good writer?" The answer: "Just sit down at your desk, open your heart and discover that inner authenticity!"

ACQUIRING EXECUTIVE INTELLIGENCE IN TEN (NOT-SO-EASY) STEPS

Acquiring the attributes of executive intelligence can take a lifetime of concerted effort with occasional lapses and wrong turns, hopefully followed by new learning and corrections. The most marvelous aspect of human behavior is our ability to master sound judgment—the most challenging human task as well. Even the best of us—captains of industry, national leaders, celebrities—suffer from occasional lapses in social judgment. How we recover and learn from our errors makes us who we are in the eyes of society.

If you're willing to put in the time and effort—typically years rather than months—and if you're willing to discover your inner, authentic self, then you can begin to acquire those marvelous traits of an emotionally intelligent executive that will earn you the respect and success you deserve. The following sections describe these attributes.

1. Nonjudgmental Attitude: Bringing Out the Best in Others

The first attribute of the emotionally intelligent executive is a nonjudgmental attitude to all staff members. This means, first and foremost, accepting each individual on the basis of what he or she offers at the present moment, not on what others think may have happened in the past (with all the gossip and judgment that come through the grapevine).

Nonjudgmental executives look at each person first of all with courtesy and respect, with an attitude of concern and support. They consider each first meeting an honor, approaching the other person with openness to the potential of a new relationship.

Consider that the opposite of a nonjudgmental attitude is self-righteousness. From a self-righteous point of view, everything becomes the fault of the other. Where nonjudgment is accompanied by compassion, self-righteousness comes with fear and suspicion. An executive of the old school in self-righteous mode has no consideration for the feelings of others, or at best is somewhat aware of the feelings of others. The emotionally intelligent executive, preparing for the twenty-first century, is effective not only in making others feel special, but also in encouraging them to reach for the best they can be.

2. Perceptiveness: Helping Others to Understand Themselves

Emotionally intelligent executives are perceptive, and are effective in communicating this. They understand others and, with the wisdom of their experience, help them understand themselves, with the feeling that they are appreciated. This perceptive quality comes about from identifying with others' feelings, by walking in another's shoes, by understanding in the literal sense of "standing under" the other's perspective.

Perceptiveness grows slowly over time as this domain of awareness is explored. With the sincere intention to help others understand themselves, this ability to see things through others' eyes can be acquired. Only by coming from the inner serenity of a "quiet heart" can one be truly perceptive of others' feelings and intentions.

At worst, the old-style executive is totally unaware of others' feelings, although may occasionally listen and hear what others express. Emotionally intelligent executives, however, perceive others' feelings so clearly that they can assist others in a deeper understanding of themselves.

3. Sincerity: Fostering Genuine Honesty

Sincerity is the third trait, which involves being honest about one's own feelings and intentions.

Some time ago, I was lucky enough to hear a live performance by Doc Watson, a preeminent American folk singer/guitarist, now in his 70s. Mr. Watson is totally blind, yet so clear about his intentions that he virtually sheds a light in front of himself for those intentions to occur. Before the break, for example, as the applause for his flat-picking genius subsided, he declared, in a very matter-of-fact manner, exactly where he'd be leaving the stage and precisely how he'd be doing it. The assistance he required followed smoothly. There was no fumbling or awkwardness.

In a similar manner, by being very clear about intentions, the emotionally intelligent executive can obtain the support and assistance that pave the path for corporate goals to be attained with what seems like minimal effort.

By being authentic, frank and forthright, the emotionally intelligent executive articulates goals clearly and precisely. There is no deceit, pretense or hypocrisy. The private person is essentially the same as the public personality—natural and genuine. Spontaneous feelings are warmly and heartily expressed.

This trait can be learned by articulating one's feelings more often, more accurately, and more publicly, carefully tempered with sensitivity as to effect. This is where some of the open-hearted authenticity comes into play.

At worst, the outmoded executives' words bear no relation to their feelings. Some may be genuine on occasion but do not always say what they really mean. The emotionally intelligent executive, however, is deeply genuine and spontaneous in expression of true feeling. When conflict occurs, she is always open to resolving it by giving priority to understanding the facts and human feelings leading up to the conflict.

4. Presence: Taking Personal Responsibility

The fourth trait can best be characterized by the term "openness," to whatever facts or feelings present themselves at any given moment. Even when feelings get overheated, an open attitude can help those who are upset to express their emotions in working toward an ultimate resolution.

Emotionally intelligent executives deal directly with the problems that fall under their levels of responsibility, and make direct contact with the individuals most involved. They do not delegate high-priority problems or procrastinate in dealing with them. They make themselves available as soon as possible, not next week or "when I get around to it." They get first-hand, direct knowledge of the factors leading up to the problem and use their perceptions of others to come to a resolution as quickly as possible. They listen to all parties who can provide useful information and leave the door open for further communication.

They do not decide or conclude until all parties have had an opportunity to argue their case, and are open to all perspectives. They are willing to make exceptions to policy in order to facilitate the uncovering of important information that might contribute to a resolution, even if that means putting off regularly scheduled meetings if the urgency of the problem requires it.

As soon as possible, they will make the new findings known to the organization's members in as candid and honest a manner as is possible. It is such candor at critical times that makes for a high level of trust and respect for the administration as a whole.

Outmoded executives avoid problems either by delegating them or by procrastination. Some executives deal with problems by being present yet allowing others to solve the problem while they observe, maintaining a cautious distance. The emotionally intelligent executive, however, gets directly involved and takes personal responsibility for both favorable and unfavorable aspects of the problem and its resolution. As Harry S. Truman, one of our more open-minded presidents put it so succinctly, "The buck stops here!"

5. Relevance: Supporting the Truth

The fifth quality is relevance, referring to the ability to deal with the what, where, why, who and how of any situation—the concrete facts that describe goals, problems and solutions. As we know, "the devil is in the details," and an executive who can deal with relevant, specific details will always have a better handle on any situation. An executive who can get others to focus on the relevant details of challenges at hand will be more successful more often, more quickly.

The executive with relevance bears upon a problem directly with exploration of pertinent facts, is sensitive to germane issues, and is particularly open to suitable suggestions. He is particularly sensitive to making the best pairing between employees and the projects to which they're best suited. Executives with relevance have the ability to bring different factions together to focus directly on the challenges at hand, to form clarity out of chaos. They can make the complex and murky become clear and channeled toward sometimes surprisingly elegant solutions, glean specific facts from those who try to hide behind generalities and abstractions. They can add quantitative numbers to qualitative substance, separate fact from speculation. Ultimately, they can solidify the efforts of others to bring their energies to bear on high-priority challenges, and guide them to fruition.

The outmoded executive passively allows those hiding behind abstract generalizations to lead all others astray, without intervening. The emotionally intelligent executive, however, demands specifics, supporting those who explore the truth in detail.

6. Expressiveness: Creating Smooth Communication

Next is the quality of being personable. The old-style executives were dour and expressionless, probably convinced that a display of humanity would be seen as a sign of weakness. The emotionally intelligent executive is the opposite, pulsing with vibrant personality. She tends to be open and forthright, yet governed by a clear sense of propriety, measuring the effects of personal expression on the audience at all times.

The purpose of self-expression is not to find an audience for each and every whim and opinion but rather to encourage others to higher levels of energy and dedication. By selective sharing of personal feelings and opinions, the executive can forge a stronger sense of group identity, proving herself as a secure leader to whom others can look for inspiration and support. By being sensitive to the issues of the surrounding corporate culture, the emotionally intelligent executive can articulate those concerns in a personally involved context and draw others in to feel personally involved as well.

By fostering an attractively warm and expressive personality, an executive can make others feel more accepted and involved. By being open as to overall philosophy and values, she can guide others guilelessly in those directions, as well as create a general attitude of smooth and open communication.

Outmoded executives appear completely uninvolved and impersonal, and keep others unaware of their personal philosophy. They may appear personable but are hardly ever specific about personal values or philosophy. The emotionally intelligent executive, however, comes across as a highly unique individual because of the ongoing, candid expression of personal feelings, guided by the overriding criteria of relevance and fruitfulness.

7. Supportiveness: Fostering Loyalty and a Sense of Contribution

In addition to being personable, the emotionally intelligent executive is supportive. In addition to sharing personal feelings and opinions, he makes people feel more than adequate, that they are unique individuals contributing significantly to the corporate cause. This is done through nonverbal as well as verbal means. Tone of voice, eye contact, facial expression, warm handshakes and pats on the back all have a place in communicating warmth and acceptance.

Sensitive to issues of sexual harassment, the executive is crystal clear about personal boundaries and never, never allows any misinterpretation of nonverbal signs of acceptance. He is extremely sensitive to personal boundaries in every respect. Purity of heart and clarity of intent should leave no room for misunder-standings in this very sensitive area.

The emotionally intelligent executive can bring forth an excit-ing, vigorous and colorful personality when that is called for, and this cannot be achieved without the nonverbal component of expressing warmth and acceptance. Enthusiasm and zeal can be encouraged by such display of personality, and it's up to the executive to encourage such excitement among those in his sphere of responsibility.

In addition to expressing acceptance and support, the emo-tionally intelligent executive is authentic in occasionally express-ing forceful and even angry feelings, although in moderation. Otherwise, he can be seen as disingenuous and insincere. No one who is genuine can avoid at least the occasional expression of feelings of anger and frustration.

Overall, an executive must stand as a durable figure of strength, withstanding all attempts at undermining the power inherent in the position, through thick and thin, through manip-ulative favor-seeking and malicious gossip. One way of garner-ing support is by offering it, because giving support engenders support in return. This offer can take the form of encouragement and personal as well as internal political support. Funding is another way to offer support, as is protecting others' reputations against malevolent gossip. Loyalty is a mutual process—the more you give, the more you receive. Support can also take the form of public awards and honors for tasks well accomplished. The support that wears well over time, however, is more likely to be private, personal encouragement and comfort in times of personal trials and tribulations.

Outmoded executives come across as impersonal and unin-volved, devoid of consideration of others' feelings, although the better ones can occasionally show concern and support for others. The emotionally intelligent executive is both understand-ing and compassionate and this comes through clearly in all transactions, through verbal and nonverbal expression.

8. Boldness: Resolving Conflicts Early

The next quality has to do with being candidly challenging when appropriate, without being abrasive. This may be necessary when there is a clear discrepancy between a job requirement and its current performance.

In the face of any important discrepancy, either between job and performance or between factions, the emotionally intelligent executive will invite the individual or parties to respond to the specifics of the discrepancy. She takes the initiative in confronting such discrepancies even before others take notice of them, and listens to relevant facts without bias. The executive's response is candid and forthright, offering the benefit of doubt freely and with support. The resolution will be understood clearly by all concerned. The mission of the executive is to emerge with the solution that harms the least and best supports corporate direction and philosophy.

The emotionally intelligent executive approaches each situation boldly and does not put up with nonsense. She reacts to attempts at deceit and evasiveness with calmness and matches strength with those who would be untruthful, persevering in the pursuit of honesty. The ultimate result is truth, hopefully achieved with mutual respect and propriety, resorting to a display of angry confrontation only in those exceptional cases that require it.

Forcing others to confront their discrepancies can result in crises, characterized by fear, anger and resentment. The emotionally intelligent executive's initial approach, however, is gentle and warm, hoping to stave off personal vendettas. There is a talent to keeping negative emotions at bay during such crises. Some have that talent well developed.

The outmoded executive avoids discrepancies, hoping they'll disappear with time, that no one will notice them, or that others will step in and resolve them. She deals with them only at the last moment when they become unavoidable. The emotionally intelligent executive has a constant eye open for any discrepancies and attends to them at the earliest opportunity, approaching each one initially with warmth and sensitivity.

9. Zeal: Offering a Model for Effective Leadership

Ultimately, the emotionally intelligent executive brings to fruition the sum of inner potential, so that all efforts expended are put to fully effective use. Conflicts and problems are dealt with as early as possible. Since personal skills and talents are utilized fully, work is experienced as personally fulfilling and satisfying. Such executives enjoy offering a leadership role for their subordinates to admire and emulate. They make use of and enjoy every working moment, even the more challenging ones. They feel intensely involved throughout the day, being sensitive both to their own inner feelings and the feelings of those around them.

They enjoy their abilities to influence and persuade others. They enjoy being part of the solution, impressing others with their ability to make things happen. They enjoy being bottom-line people, taking satisfaction in concrete results.

Despite the intensity of their personalities, they can maintain an inner calm that counterbalances their spontaneous expressiveness. They have the ability to see situations from different perspectives, avoiding black-and-white, dichotomous thinking. They encourage others to have open minds and to join them in taking more responsibility.

The outmoded executive feels ineffectual, lacks a personal philosophy, has low self-esteem and is cautiously guarded. The emotionally intelligent executive has a healthy self-regard and feels competent in accomplishing most challenges. He is keenly aware of the effects of all personal expression and is open to all "gut" feelings. Although fully enjoying executive privilege, he is not addicted to such power and finds deeper fulfillment in more personal relationships. He can make a clear distinction between need and greed. Need is easily fulfilled, greed is never satisfied.

Awareness of one's own human vulnerability counterbalances a sense of personal power in order to maintain a sense of personal humility. Ultimately, the emotionally intelligent executive is responsible to himself or herself more than to any other person. The burden is great, but carried with inner serenity.

10. Self-Assurance: Encouraging Others to Greater Levels of Risk-Taking and Achievement

Finally, there is the quality of self-assurance that singles out the emotionally intelligent executive. The self-confident executive makes others feel calm and assured about their own roles, encouraging them to dig deeper into their personal resources to get the job done. By being warmly expressive and intensely involved in helping others, emotionally intelligent executives encourage others to greater levels of risk-taking and achievement.

Confident in their own abilities, comfortable in their moral convictions and secure in their social standing, emotionally intelligent executives have a strong and effective presence. Their primary consideration is to empower those who trust them, and this they can do through eloquent persuasion. Through their vigorous, spirited personality they're able to influence and to convince others with a sense of authority, without giving up their intellectual integrity.

The outmoded executive hides anxiety by appearing expressionless, inhibited and insecure. The emotionally intelligent executive, facing the twenty-first century boldly, exudes self-confidence and puts a high priority on ongoing support of others. She is highly self-expressive and has the ability to communicate effectively.

CONCLUSION

The emotionally intelligent executive knows the difference between offering a hungry person a fish and teaching the art of fishing, and chooses the latter. He knows the difference between form and substance, and prefers the latter. He knows the value of time, how quickly it passes, and chooses to spend it wisely as experiments in truth. The ultimate question guiding his behavior is "Will this do good for others?"

If any new form of management is going to take hold, it's got to start at the top, or at least find adequate acceptance there; otherwise it's likely to fail before long. In the next chapter we'll see how successful leaders approach management through effective delegation as they head into the next century, and how successful executives negotiate with emotional intelligence in the global marketplace.

11

Delegating and Negotiating with Executive Intelligence

> Great presidents don't do great things. Great presidents get a
> lot of other people to do great things.
>
> —PRESIDENT CLINTON, quoted in *Time* magazine

Why is delegation such an important priority as we enter the
twenty-first century? With increasing technology making possible more work in less time, time is at a greater and greater
premium. Executive responsibilities have multiplied to the point
where delegation is essential. The worst thing you can do as an
executive, however, is to leave your staff with the impression
that you're loading them down with mundane tasks while you
are busy striving for individual glory.

DELEGATION

When accomplished with executive intelligence, delegation can
be an opportunity for growth for both you and your staff. When

delegating a task, first seek the staff member's perspective of the challenge at hand. Then offer detailed information to provide a clear picture of the ultimate objectives. The lack of detailed information necessary for implementation is the cause of most frustration with delegated tasks. The executive should always offer to be a resource to assist the staff member when necessary, creating a sense of team effort and support.

The more assignments you delegate, the more you can utilize the increased time available to concentrate on the most critical task of long-term planning and growth. Other time can be spent dealing with crises, visiting sites where delegated assignments are being completed to review progress and communicating with upper management or board members.

Emotionally intelligent delegation involves clear communication of the following:

1. Precise initiation and completion dates
2. How the assignment fits into overall goals
3. A clear channel of communication with you to get information or to suggest required modifications
4. Other resources you know of that can be helpful
5. Problems that have arisen with such tasks in the past
6. The limit of authority (the point at which you wish to be notified)
7. The criteria for evaluating success at completion

By providing this clear information up front, fear and uncertainty are significantly diminished. By providing an overall perspective, the staff members get a sense of the importance of the assignment, and this enhances their self-esteem. With clear limits of authority and criteria for evaluation, the staff members now have a better idea of how they fit into the larger picture. They can appreciate that contribution with a greater sense of security, which will in turn form the basis of a sense of mission you can bring to the project.

Delegating effectively involves the emotionally intelligent awareness of each team member's strengths and weaknesses, and taking time to communicate clearly, leaving the lines of communication open, even if your schedule is very tight.

The emotionally intelligent executive delegates effectively to free up time for dealing with far-reaching and complex long-term issues that cannot be handled by the self-managed teams. The aim is to create a smooth-running, efficient enterprise that fosters the growth of its team members. At its best, such an enterprise will not only be highly profitable, as all resources are being used to their fullest potential, but will also assure excellence in quality, motivation for its team members and direction for organizational growth.

In order to delegate in an emotionally intelligent manner, consider the following seven guidelines:

1. Reflect on the directions you want your company and your team leaders to take before initiating any projects or changes.

2. Make sure your team leaders understand the sense of direction you've come up with. Clarify your objectives.

3. Set priorities clearly when delegating assignments.

4. Maintain open communication with those under your direction but not in a manner giving the impression that you're checking up on them.

5. Encourage your team leaders to communicate with you as they implement your objectives in their own areas of competence.

6. Delegate assignments in such a way that your staff is sufficiently familiar with the overall details to take over your role at a moment's notice if that were necessary.

7. Delegate in such a way that you end up trusting that it'll get done even if you never get involved till completion.

Although emotionally intelligent delegation takes a good deal of thought and consideration, such energy is well spent. As a busy executive you may enjoy assuming responsibilities single-handedly, but resist the impulse for self-gratification. By learning to delegate projects more readily, you can gain the time necessary to acquire a larger perspective, so essential if the company is to be kept on the right course. Fostering the growth of staff for their own welfare, you can train individuals to improve in their competence even if you realize that you're able to manage projects more competently at the present time. As your time is precious, take the opportunity to delegate today. This is the only certain way to save time in the future.

A sense of trust can be gained through emotionally honest communication and by focusing on the outcome of the assignment rather than the mechanics of it. Beyond that, when things go wrong, demand accountability in private while assuming responsibility in public. After all, the ultimate responsibility is yours. Assume that mistakes will happen from time to time. See them as opportunities for learning, not only for your staff, but as opportunities for you to fine-tune your own skills of delegation.

Ultimately, emotionally intelligent delegation hinges on open communication. This enables you to know your staff members, to know in which directions they can grow to reach their hidden potential, for that is where they will shine, and the whole enterprise will benefit. The New Team Ethic is about personal fulfillment. Fulfill your staff members' needs and your organization will move to the next level of excellence.

EMOTIONALLY INTELLIGENT NEGOTIATION

Win/win negotiation is the only kind of negotiation that works in the long run, as we've learned over the years. Unless both sides gain substantial benefit in any new agreement, there's bound to be renewed conflict sooner rather than later.

The old style of negotiation involved playing hardball—a macho approach with intimidation and forcefulness as key strategies. Emotionally intelligent negotiation has more to do with flexibility and an attitude of mutual benefit.

An approach of greater openness and integrity of character has become increasingly important. With increased communication potential through high-tech information processing and the need for synergy in an increasingly global marketplace, negotiation has become much more sophisticated and personalized. People—and their feelings—count more than ever. Macho power, the sense of victory by getting something over on the other side through deception or intimidation, is no longer appropriate. Because of more sophisticated communication technology, truth is harder to conceal these days. Clearly, trust is a greater factor in negotiations than it was in past decades. Word gets around pretty quickly these days and integrity is at great premium. Emotional intelligence in negotiating is not a luxury; it's essential.

Emotionally intelligent negotiation goes a step further. It's a whole new way of coming to resolution—a proactive approach that maximizes the probability of success—for *both* sides!

Let's take a look at two aspects of emotionally intelligent negotiation: first, in an at-home, informal situation, and then in a more complex business setting.

Domestic "Warm-Up"

Imagine yourself in a familiar household setting. You've contracted with a painter, referred by his mother, an acquaintance at church. "Oh, he's a real professional," she's promised you, with unquestionable sincerity.

The painter—let's call him Paul—in fact has never made any responsible decisions about house painting. Oh, he's a painter all right, just as his mother promised, but he's always worked for others, where he received detailed instructions. And so Paul didn't bother to test the existing paint to determine whether it was latex or oil based before purchasing all the paint supplies. Of course, they turned out to be the wrong type.

So now, you find out, the paint job is worthless. What you considered a bargain at $2,000 is worse than useless.

Paul denies responsibility, insisting you should have told him about the existing paint. You soon realize that assuming responsibility is not his mainstay. And you can't afford to make an enemy of his mother. So you're in a fix. Stopping the check you gave him just yesterday will only cause further misunderstanding, hostility and possibly a minor lawsuit. So you've got no choice but to negotiate. What a wonderful opportunity to learn!

Here are six principles of emotionally intelligent negotiation you can now use for this fairly domestic problem, which apply just as aptly to the more complex corporate setting. If it works here, it'll certainly work there.

1. *Tell the truth, the whole truth and nothing but the truth in explaining your position at the outset.*
"Paul, we had an agreement that you would complete the job of painting my home for $2,000. Now I've discovered that you used the wrong paint."

2. *In your honest presentation, be sure to include how you feel about the situation.*
"I feel taken advantage of and frustrated."

3. *Avoid any emotional issues that are tangential to the issue at hand.*
It would be tempting to say, "Paul, I've known your mother a long time and she's a sweet, honest woman. How dare you con her into thinking you knew all about painting houses when all this time you've just been working for others who've been telling you exactly what to do!"

All these tangential, though perhaps accurate, incidental facts will just stir up more hostility and make it impossible to resolve an already complex disagreement. So as Jack Webb of "Dragnet" fame would put it, "Just stick to the facts."

4. *Work for the future, not the present.*
Focusing on the present moment only, you might relieve your frustration most readily by verbally (or physically!) beating up on Paul. But beyond that shallow satisfaction, what would you have accomplished? Merely an exacerbation of the existing problem, and the likelihood of a lawsuit or two. Instead, look into the future and decide whether you want a relationship with Paul, or his mother.

If you don't want a relationship with Paul, then it's still in your best interest to resolve any dispute peaceably. Otherwise the relationship will drag on and on. Lawsuits have been known to last for years. How can you get this over with cleanly and quickly? Only by assuring that Paul is as happy about the final resolution as you are.

Thus, for the best solution, think into the future, not on the present moment. Whether you want a satisfactory relationship with your counterpart or none at all, you're best off resolving matters as peaceably as possible.

5. *Decide clearly what you really want to take away from this negotiation.*
In this imaginary conflict, what is the most important issue for you—money, pride, principle, sense of conquest? Conquest for the sake of conquest is infantile, unless you're engaged in a game with agreed-upon rules. Fighting for principle can be self-defeating, unless the principle in question is of such high priority to you it is worth fighting for.

When you argue that the paint job is worthless, Paul retorts that he spent $500 on it.

"Well, then show me the receipt!" you insist.

"No, I won't." counters Paul. "That's not your affair as to how much I paid. That's *my* business and you have no right to it!"

"You won't show it to me," you ask in amazement, "on principle?!"

"Call it what you will," Paul rails defensively. "You have no right to see it!"

Is that principle worth fighting for? I don't think so. As in most situations, what at first sounds like high principle turns out to be stubborn pride.

Whether money is worth fighting for depends on too many factors to make any general statements about it. However, responsibility and liability in contractual agreements are generally measured in dollars and cents, although reputation is also a big factor.

So, as you enter into any negotiation, decide beforehand what it is you want to come away with. Take the time to think about it clearly and objectively. If it's money, then decide on the amount at which you're willing to take a stand. It's important to think long and hard about a stand—or lose the contest.

If the most important factor is not money, then decide there too where you will draw the line. Later on, you may negotiate for some other factor, but for the time being, it's essential you know what's most important to you before you start negotiating—don't try to figure it out in the actual process of negotiation.

6. *Try to appreciate what the other party wants to get out of this negotiation.*
The best way to understand what the other party wants is to ask. And keep asking as the negotiations proceed.

Imagine you were dividing a pie in two and the other party could choose which half he wants. Your best strategy is to cut the pie as close to equal as possible, since you'll surely get the smaller piece. That's the best strategy for emotionally intelligent negotiation.

Now, let's see how these principles apply in a business setting.

Down to Business

Emotionally intelligent negotiation involves not only awareness of feelings, your own as well as those of the other party; it also requires proper preparation.

"Count the beans" accurately beforehand. In other words, do your homework on the numbers involved, so that there is a minimum of fumbling when you need to be concentrating on interpersonal dynamics. Likewise, get your legal and technical background information down pat for the same reason. Do all your homework on financial, legal and technical aspects so you can concentrate more fully on your emotional intelligence. For example, find out from your legal experts whether legal issues might come into play. If so, study the ramifications.

Get to know as much as possible about your counterpart. Collect as much public information as possible about the company, including, if appropriate, information on wages and overhead, staff training, warehousing and distribution network, market share and customer base. What are the corporate policies and procedures of your counterpart? Find out the company's experience with unions, if appropriate, its policy toward quality assurance, its history of penalties of breach of contract, if any.

Be prepared to put in at least two to four hours of preparation for every projected hour of actual negotiation process. The more preparation time you put in, the better your chances of success in negotiation. Spend some of this preparation time getting to know the personalities who'll be facing you across the table— official function, level of education, competence, and to whom each individual reports.

Beyond that, do your homework about yourself and the logical parameters of your negotiations. What are your priorities? What is your bottom line on the various issues under negotiation? Where can you afford to compromise the most? What counter-arguments can you anticipate before you even sit down at the table? What alternatives can you come up with in response? What expert information might be of help to you?

Also, spend some time anticipating the emotional makeup of the individuals you're going to meet across the table as well as the ramifications of their corporate culture (see the section on "Cultural Intelligence" later in the chapter).

Make sure that all logistical details are taken care of beforehand: location, seating arrangements, invitations, agenda, transportation, housing, meals and communication technology. Check supporting documents, notes, statistics and audio-visual materials. Make sure that there are sufficient handout materials.

Once you have made your preparations, you are ready to put the six principles of emotionally intelligent negotiation into action.

1. *Begin by explaining your position honestly and forthrightly.*
Of course, don't start with the most important items. That will make things too intense too quickly. Instead, begin with items on which you can compromise readily. That will get you off on a cooperative footing.

As you build toward the more important items, go into the particulars to nail down as many specifics as possible. The more important it is to you, the more you want the details locked in. Be honest about what you want so the other side will have more time to accommodate your needs. Your ongoing honesty will convince the other side of your genuineness and increase their trust level. If an issue becomes deadlocked, let it go for the time being. Come back to it when the mood lightens up and every-one's in a more compromising mood. Save your intensity for the end, if that becomes necessary, to resolve conflict in areas of key importance to you. With more invested on both sides, resolution is more likely.

2. *Include your feelings in your presentation.*
By being honest from the get-go, you can more easily afford to be emotionally open as well. You build trust by such openness and increase the likelihood of openness and honesty from the other side. You can continue to present yourself from a position of strength rather than fear since you don't have to worry about any cover-up.

3. *Avoid tangential emotional issues.*
During ordinary negotiations, it's easy to get caught up in emotional issues that have little to do with matters that really count. When conflict steams up, emotions can become chaotic. By sticking to your agenda, this can be avoided. Be firm on this point. If the other side insists with heated stubbornness to pursue an irrelevant issue, be prepared to walk out for some breathing space to cool down. Only do this if there's no alternative, but when you do walk out, do so resolutely and politely. Since you've been open and honest, your readiness to walk out will have more effect and you'll probably be called back before you get out the door.

By being honest and avoiding tangential emotional issues, conflict will be minimized. This, in conjunction with your readiness to walk out if things go awry, will reduce the likelihood of your side being intimidated.

4. *Work for the future as well as for the present.*
If success is to be durable, you need to look to the future to anticipate what might go wrong and address those items fully. Consider quality as well as quantity, terms of payment and delivery as well as warranties.

Make sure the compromises you've worked out will be sufficient for the other side in the long run as well.

5. *State clearly what you want to take away from this negotiation.*
Know clearly how far you're willing to compromise on the various issues. For each item, determine your bottom line early, so that you can focus on being emotionally intelligent about the other side of the table instead of figuring out your bottom line during negotiation itself.

That way, you can be more sensitive to where the bottom line is for the other side. If you've done more homework, and you stay emotionally intelligent to their process, you're more likely to come out successfully.

6. *Ask for and appreciate the other side's needs, and keep this in mind for the duration of the negotiations.*
Emotionally intelligent negotiation works best in the long run because it's more honest and operates on the basis of mutual respect and support. Such negotiations are difficult enough without attempts at deception and one-upmanship. You and your counterparts are in this for the long term. You want to build trust over time and this is an excellent opportunity.

Ultimately, you're looking for the ideal fit between your needs and the other side's needs given the resources available. Having stated your position openly and clearly from the beginning, spend the rest of the time doing more listening than speaking. Your job is to understand the other side's needs almost as well as your own and act as a broker between the two sides rather than an advocate for your side alone. Paradoxically, this emotionally intelligent approach will get you much more than if you bargained offensively.

CULTURAL INTELLIGENCE

Emotionally intelligent negotiation also involves a sensitivity to cultural differences. As the global network of corporate business becomes increasingly accessible, you are more and more likely to be dealing with officers and executives from different cultures. This requires cultural intelligence as well as emotional intelligence. Cultural intelligence allows you to accommodate your cultural counterparts in personal matters such as language, dietary considerations and even behavioral habits. You need to learn what phrases or idioms might be inappropriate, what foods are proper to recommend and how to greet and meet in a manner that will not be seen as insulting or disrespectful. Japanese corporate types, for example, value politeness very highly and are extremely concerned about "saving face." Their preferred form of greeting is a bow from the waist. The individual of lower status typically matches the bow of the higher status individual with a deeper, or lower, bow. If they come to visit your country, a firm handshake can follow the custom of bowing.

Although the Japanese enjoy receiving gifts, particularly brandy, the Chinese do not, and might become embarrassed by gifts of great value. When dining out with Chinese and Japanese, however, it would be wise to at least give the old college try at using chopsticks, before resorting to more Western utensils.

When visiting the Middle East, don't be surprised if your male counterpart offers to kiss you. A typical greeting there is a kiss on both cheeks. In Arab countries, avoid mentioning alcohol and, in Israel and Arab countries, don't ever ask for pork. Just a couple of words will take you far in gaining acceptance from your hosts. In Israel, the word "shalom," meaning "peace," can be used as a greeting both on first meeting and on departure. In Arab countries, the word "Inshallah" ("God willing") appropriately inserted into your negotiations can help immeasurably.

European businesspeople tend to be a bit more formal than their American counterparts, as are our Canadian neighbors. First-name familiarity comes a bit more slowly in Canada and much more slowly in Europe. In both areas, men's suitcoats are slower to come off than in the States.

Arabs and South Americans have this in common: They have a concept of personal space that is different from ours. If you find them "in your face" as they speak with you, don't back up to resume your usual personal space. That might be considered an insult.

As an emotionally intelligent negotiator, you need to be sensitive to regional differences within the United States itself. For example, Manhattan and Los Angeles make for an interesting contrast. Both are highly unique and well known across the world as business centers, but that's probably the extent of the similarity. In Manhattan, the pace is fast and the written contract is king. In L.A., on the other hand, the pace is slower and trust based on personal relationships comes before signatures on contracts.

In Manhattan, family life and business life are kept separate for the most part. In L.A., they overlap and outdoor activities (boating, skiing, golf) are possible sites of informal negotiation. Home visits are more likely on the West Coast as well.

Like those in Los Angeles, people in Atlanta, Georgia, tend to cultivate relationships of trust prior to finalizing contractual agreements. A faith in genuine honesty, often considered naive in New York, is often paramount in Atlanta, especially among native Georgians.

In the Northwest, cities such as Seattle and Portland are taking on California values as more and more Los Angelenos take up residence in Washington and Oregon. This is a region of contrasts—locals versus newcomers, environmentalists versus technology advocates, humid coast weather versus the desert-like eastern side of the mountains, Oriental trade versus local California expertise and, finally, rain versus sun. When negotiating in this region, expect the unexpected, but enjoy its diversity.

Finally, for a more laid-back approach to negotiations, you might find yourself lucky enough to travel to Hawaii. Diversity is rampant there too, but for the most part, on a more integrated basis. American-born Japanese and Koreans make up a significant slice of the population and American-born Chinese are heavily involved in Hawaiian commerce. There is a strong native Hawaiian cultural influence, though native Hawaiians are not typically in positions of control.

Overall, the Hawaiian pace is very slow. Dress is quite informal and suits and ties are of little importance. The challenge of negotiating in Hawaii arises from the fact that trust is based on long-term relationships and newcomers need to exercise a bit of patience until they find acceptance. Enjoying local customs—accepting and wearing flower leis, eating poi (mashed taro root with a somewhat bland, pasty taste to the novice), and attempting the hula dance—will endear you to the Hawaiian's heart and hasten your acceptance.

CONCLUSION

The art of delegating is a balancing act that requires very fine judgment. The emotionally intelligent executive tends to delegate so she can concentrate on long-term planning and growth, choosing those to assume responsibility incisively, with an eye to developing unique talents, keeping a trusting and supportive eye on the delegated projects.

Emotionally intelligent negotiation, beyond win/win negotiation, involves awareness in depth of the other company's culture, especially if that organization is not domestic, and an emotional openness that invites the other party to be forthright as well. Beyond success for the moment, it builds toward the future, inviting future cooperation and possible integration of complementary products or services.

Cooperation of this sort becomes more likely as barriers between domestic and foreign companies disappear with the growth of the global marketplace. In the next chapter, we'll discover the secret of Japan's success in jumping ahead of the West in terms of applying executive intelligence and how we need to stay globally sensitive as well as open to all voices in our own corporate communities.

Part IV
Becoming Emotionally Intelligent

"Reminds me of comic book teams of heroes," I remember with a smile, "where each character is a very unique individual, but each member's strength comes out fully so the team as a whole is invincible. Sports teams, too, I guess, at least the ones that excel."

"Interesting comparison, David. I don't recall such comic books, so I'll take your word for it."

"Carl, what needs do you see the individuals in a team having? I mean, is emotional openness and dealing with conflict all there is to it?"

"Well, let's think it through. Team needs are probably the same as those typical for people in general, in groups or not. Some people get meaning from proving themselves capable, taking on tough challenges and succeeding. Others may be less driven but need to feel accepted and liked by others."

"You mean like me?" I ask with a smile, remembering Carl's astute questions that touched me earlier.

"Perhaps," says Carl, then moves on with his analysis. "Others find meaning when they're in charge of others and enjoy the trappings of leadership."

"The opposite of you, you mean?"

Ignoring me, Carl charges right on. "Then there are those who seem to find security in mastering the details of a job. Somehow it makes them feel safe to know that the 'i's are dotted and the 't's are crossed."

"So which are you?"

Carl is silent, reflecting. "I'm not much for self-analysis. What's your opinion?"

"Well, I'm not much for being judgmental, so how 'bout we try on each for size? Let's see . . . you enjoy the challenge of developing theories of human communication. You enjoy getting close to others through your caring way of counseling and we've already determined that you don't enjoy being in charge of others. You don't strike me as being overly concerned with details, so I guess overall you enjoy challenging work and you also find it important to be close to others."

"Well, David, hearing you go through the options, I'm most likely to agree with the challenge of work. I don't mind being alone, actually, although I do enjoy helping people very much."

"I guess the best team would have a little of each, so that all the functions get taken care of. Let's see . . . there's taking on the challenge of the job, ensuring group cohesion by making members feel open to each other, making sure the 'i's are dotted and the 't's are crossed and, let's see, what else?"

"You forgot about the bossy type," chuckles Carl.

"Oh yes, is there a place for that in our team of equals?"

"Good question," responds Carl. "I really don't know. I imagine someone would eventually have to be considered the leader, someone to make sure that . . ."

"That everything hangs together," I come in quickly. "But not necessarily the type of boss we usually think of. I guess he could be a focal point for the group, as much as secretary or clerk as a bossy, commander type."

"Or he might be the most sensitive in the group," suggests Carl.

"Or the most verbal one. I guess there's no clear-cut type to be in charge of such a group."

"I think that's it," Carl's voice is excited once again. "That's what makes these groups so darn interesting. They don't fit a simple mold. Each group has its own unique characteristics and so will the leadership. That's what I find so fascinating about the whole thing. Such effective groups, and especially their leadership functions, however they've worked out, are always of interest to me. I find I always have something to learn from them. One thing I tend to find in such groups, that always pulls me to them, is the sense of enthusiasm that drives them."

12

Innovation— East and West

O, East is East, and West is West, and never the twain shall meet.

—RUDYARD KIPLING

Why do the Japanese seem to be ahead of us in applying executive intelligence to the workplace? And why has their rate of productivity exceeded that of the United States by 400 percent since World War II? The answer, in essence, is the Japanese version of self-managed teams. Whereas Americans have struggled with employee/employer problems through union-management dialectics for so many years, the Japanese have used their cultural history of feudal loyalty to business advantage.

Developing an enlightened version of their feudal society, Japanese corporations enjoy pervasively organic structures— organizations in which all members fit in a very personal and intricate way—so that both the individual and the corporation benefit.

JAPAN'S FOCUS ON COMMUNITY AND LOYALTY

One of the characteristics of this highly efficient, monolithically structured system is a strong sense of loyalty and trust. This enables Japanese companies to extend their sales forces far beyond the shores of their island nation and still maintain a strong, clear communication that helps make this international enterprise highly competitive.

The individual Japanese corporation is part of the network of Japanese companies that share a chauvinistic style of integrating their respective resources to make "battle" with foreign industry. The combination of intense loyalty within companies and the chauvinistically based trust level among them makes for a very formidable economic force in the international marketplace.

Compare this to the traditionally structured American company, with relatively little communication between management and labor, to its Japanese counterpart, where each worker is well integrated with the higher levels of management. Clearly, knowing the strengths and weaknesses of each employee makes for greater efficiency at job assignment. Only as American companies shift to an emotionally intelligent style will they begin to comprehend what the Japanese have known for a long time, the importance of interpersonal sensitivity. As complex as each work setting is, only the Japanese and emotionally intelligent Americans can best fine-tune levels of productivity. The rest are at a clear disadvantage, for they cannot enjoy the subtlety that human closeness of self-management affords.

Emotional intelligence in the workplace fosters a sense of community, which the Japanese already have. Corporate America now has the opportunity to gain that same advantage as it forges ahead into the next century.

It is ironic that dedication to long work hours proves productive for Japan, but not for the United States. While the Japanese are devoted to their work out of a pure sense of loyalty and devotion, Americans seem to have grown away from that. They want more personal rewards. They're bitter about the effects of downsizing and about the absence of any sense of loyalty from above.

SEXISM IN JAPAN: A CULTURAL RELIC

Of course, not all is as well as it appears to be in Japan either. Sexism runs rampant there, as Japan clings to its highly sexist cultural origins. Sexism is a common thread to many cultures throughout history. The French, German, and Hebrew languages, for example, illustrate the sexism inherent in the origins of European and Semitic cultures. Sexism in Japan has endured longer than in most cultures, but can no longer be justified in the present modern era. Japanese women are slowly emerging from eons of subjugation—a slow but inexorable process.

One of the reasons layoffs are less problematic in Japan is because of the practice of hiring women to fill in the fluid buffer zone of employment that fluctuates between good and bad times. During bad economic times, when the work force must be reduced, it's widely reported that there is no reduction in the work force. That's because the women who are hired to add to the work force during good times, and are let go during bad times, are not considered part of the "real" work force by the Japanese.

But for the men and some women who are considered part of the "real" work force, the loyalty of individual for company and vice versa is unquestioned. This intense loyalty makes for a strong level of interpersonal trust and cohesion that American companies can only gain by forsaking conventional attitudes for those of the New Team Ethic.

ZAIBATSU: A RELIC THAT WORKS

Loyalty for the Japanese transcends the individual company to a block of companies that function in a highly cooperative manner. By the middle 1930s, the Japanese economy had grown so quickly that banks became the financial hubs of a group of companies. Each large bank financially fed 20 to 30 companies that worked in an organically interdependent fashion. Each block of companies, called a *zaibatsu*, represented various industrial factors—steel manufacture, shipping, insurance, and so on. In a very real sense they formed a conglomerate.

Although other countries have similar relationships between banking and industry, for example, in Germany, where banks have taken an active part in running the businesses in which they're heavily invested, nowhere is this relationship as solidly based as it is in Japan.

Although the *zaibatsu* were legally dissolved after the end of World War II, the spirit of this federation mentality survived. The most powerful faction in the Japanese economy still resides within the banking community. The height of power in Japan is the Ministry of International Trade and Industry, the ultimate regulator of Japanese commerce. And since this Ministry and most of the more powerful banks vie for graduates from the University of Tokyo, that university is the most prestigious in the country.

Despite all this prestige at the top, Japanese workers can get financial rewards based on their efforts, regardless of their place in the industrial hierarchy, but their reward is based on group, not individual, effort. So we can see two forces at work that foster loyalty—first, competition for the right employer and the loyalty once one has been placed and, second, the cohesion that comes about when one's success is dependent on team effort.

Another essential difference between American and Japanese industry is that of specialization. American industry specializes in expertise, Japanese in company loyalty. In America today, loyalty is practically frowned upon. What with downsizing and whistle-blowing, company loyalty is at an all-time low. Americans instead focus on acquiring sufficient expertise to make themselves marketable to more companies, and sometimes to many companies, as a consultant.

The Japanese, on the other hand, consider personal expertise less important and still believe in company loyalty. Within his company of employ, a Japanese worker can be moved from one area to another, where he will be trained for his new job so as to fill any need the company may see fit at that particular time.

By the time he reaches higher levels of management, group loyalty is so ingrained in the Japanese worker that upper-level decisions are typically made as a joint effort. From the entry-level worker, who has done his best to gain employment at the most prestigious company he can attain by dint of his academic studies, to the senior-level executive, who for years has seen his success tied to the group effort, the Japanese worker identifies very strongly with his company.

EXECUTIVE INTELLIGENCE: BUILT INTO THE CULTURE

In Japanese business culture, people skills are much more sensitively tuned and subtle than they are here in the United States. Anyone familiar with the painstaking care and subtlety of Japanese greeting rituals can attest to this. These skills are associated with a deeper understanding and appreciation of others' feelings, another important component of emotional intelligence.

As for the management of emotions, the Japanese are the undisputed champs. Their culture has always revered emotional self-discipline and, at one point in history, pious servitude to the feudal lord. Ritual suicide by disembowelment, as expressed in hara-kiri, or *seppuku* as the Japanese call it, was practiced until quite recently. High-ranking members of society engaged in this practice in lieu of execution to avoid disgrace—the extreme form of suffering through self-discipline.

The Japanese cope well with frustration, releasing their hostility very rarely. The famous fantasy horror comics, so popular in Japan, are perhaps one of those rare outlets. Marital discord is relatively rare in Japan, possibly because wives manage their own painful emotions so well.

Superior management skills come easier to the Japanese because of the advantage of loyalty and also because of their ability to mediate conflict in its early, subtle stages.

Japanese workers are self-motivated because of the strong influence of the peer group. "One for all and all for one," describes their collective credo. The competition for better schooling imparts a strong work ethic from a very young age. For these and other cultural reasons, the Japanese have incorporated executive intelligence into the workplace for many years.

Of course, every system has its low points, and modern-day Japan is going through one. After many years of a booming economy, Japanese banks have overextended themselves to the tune of $260 billion. Although the larger corporations—with international operations—continue to prosper, the smaller businesses—rooted to the domestic economy—are the ones feeling the crunch.

But once again the overarching rule of executive intelligence—stay honest—comes to the rescue. If the Japanese government can come through with a genuinely honest and appropriate response—*honne*, meaning "the real thing" in Japanese—as opposed to catering to special interests with phony "window dressing"—*tatemae*, meaning "pretense" in Japanese—then Japan may be able to weather the storm.

ACCELERATING INNOVATION IN A GLOBAL VILLAGE

Clearly, executive intelligence allows for a smoother communication flow and for more creative self-management. That's exactly what's needed as we move into the twenty-first century and all the uncertainty that goes with it.

Change is occurring at an accelerated pace. What used to take decades or years to change can now happen in a matter of months. Look at the revolution in communication electronics. It took decades to develop the computer to where it became an omnipresent appliance. Today no major business can survive without it and most homes and classrooms are enjoying its benefits. On a monthly, even weekly basis, we hear of improvements of this technology that continue to alter the way we do business and live our personal lives. We are hurtling down the information superhighway.

The business environment is changing more quickly than ever as well, in terms of decentralization and unencumbered global economics. Major industries have become deregulated. Unions are weaker than ever. Ownership in corporate America is moving inexorably from the hands of the few to those of the many as participatory management continues to grow and as giant corporations split into smaller, more effective, goal-focused, entities.

Marshall McLuhan's (1989) predictions of a global village are clearly coming true. With enhanced electronic communication possibilities we can "speak" with countries across the globe in real time. A fax or e-mail message from New York to Tokyo or Buenos Aires or New Delhi takes just about as little time as it does from New York to New Jersey. The stock markets of the various countries now interface electronically so that when the Tokyo exchange has indigestion, the American market burps.

Unfortunately for the United States, Japan has made better use of the emerging information superstructure by looking ahead and blending into the future. Perhaps this is because of the Japanese culture's inherent respect for emotional intelligence— managing one's emotions, being extremely sensitive to others' feelings, and being respectful of innovative feedback regardless of the status of the contributor. As a result, Japan's reputation for quality of goods has gone from post-World War II flimsy and cheap to present-day innovative and reliable. "Who really won that war?" is a question that's been asked before. Given the tremendous burden that the United States has taken on as international policeman and the resulting effect on its budget deficit, the answer is becoming even more definite.

Corporate America no longer has the luxury of conservative reactionism. Trends are cycling through at a greater frequency and with more dramatic impact. With a more emotionally intelligent approach, an attitude of strategic anticipation can replace America's more cautious stance, as recommended by Peter Drucker in his book *Managing in a Time of Great Change* (1995).

An emotionally intelligent approach to global industry would better allow for a clear understanding of how consumers perceive the innovations that overwhelm the marketplace, a more creative approach to implementation of innovations, a more productive prioritization of manufacturing resources, more creative routes of production and a more open and creative attitude to future implementation of emerging technology.

The rules of industry are changing too rapidly to be organized into any static system. Only by being open-minded and sensitive to the human process that underlies all technology can some sense of security be maintained. The pace of development is moving too quickly for theories; protocols keep changing, resisting any fixed set of conventions. Even human values have been in question in the past few years. Prejudice has given way to diversity, but its challenges persist.

LISTENING TO ALL VOICES

An emotionally intelligent approach to the challenges of rapid change allows for a faster and more flexible response to such changes. The answers can come from anywhere in the hierarchy. Only by listening to the shy and entry-level voices as well as the tried and true administrators can an industry be sure that it's tapping its resources to the best of its ability.

For every solution, new challenges arise. This is the price of such rapid technological change. Planned obsolescence is no longer necessary—it happens of its own accord. Last year's computer is already outdated, along with many of its software applications. This means an emotionally intelligent approach is not merely advantageous, it's essential! We can no longer afford to rest on the laurels of past successes. Every voice must be heard. The softest note may make all the difference in the ultimate orchestration. It took over 100,000 individuals to build the pioneering Boeing 777. Each individual played a significant role. The general manager of the entire project was executive intelligence personified, sensitive to every nuance of others' perspectives, from technician to chief pilot, and managing his own emotions impeccably.

Phrases such as "against policy" and "too radical" no longer have any place in today's marketplace. Instead we need to hear:

"What have we been doing that could be improved on?"

"Rules are made to be broken, so we're open to all suggestions."

"That suggestion sounds challenging—let's discuss it some more."

"That didn't work last time. Can we finesse it so it might work this time?"

"Sounds impossible—but intriguing. Deserves some brainstorming."

According to Walter Isaacson, who interviewed Bill Gates for a *Time* cover story, "Among Gates' favorite phrases is 'That's the stupidest thing I've ever heard,' and victims wear it as a badge of honor" (1997, p. 49).

Because an emotionally intelligent approach softens the lines of hierarchical communication, the more creative and less conventional voices can be heard. The most innovative concepts are sometimes gleaned from those least familiar with convention. Their lines of thinking are independent of what has gone on before in the company. So the newcomer is a prize of creative thought not to be overlooked.

"Bill brings to the company the idea that conflict can be a good thing," says Gates' marketing maven, Steve Ballmer. "Bill knows it's important to avoid that gentle civility that keeps you from getting to the heart of an issue quickly. He likes it when anyone, even a junior employee, challenges him, and you know he respects you when he starts shouting back" (p. 49).

Another Bill, the one in the White House, also appreciates candid feedback. According to White House reporter, Karen Breslau, "Most aides hem and haw when they disagree with the president. But if Dick Morris is to be believed, Clinton has what Morris calls 'a morbid appetite for criticism.' He likes it when people stand up to him" (1997, p. 28).

Another source of creative thought is the loner who is engrossed in a particular line of research or production and may be seen as ignorant of the big picture. Because of his idiosyncratic perspective, he's easy to ignore, but his soft voice may offer big rewards in terms of offering a new twist that may fall into the blind spot of those eyeing the bigger picture.

Rule-breakers are another source of innovation. A conservative, conventional organization would tend to undermine this individual's offerings, but an emotionally intelligent setting encouraging all voices would be more receptive to this political outsider and give such a voice equal time.

Even those suffering from the downsizing syndrome can be sources of new and usable ideas. Exit interviews can include questions regarding innovative thoughts in the individual's area of expertise. Often, the prospect of leaving brings about a bravery of its own. After all, what is there to lose at this point? If such an individual's ideas are used, he or she can ultimately be rehired, more easily outplaced, or at least given an extra bit of "transition money" to make the shift more comfortable. Exit interviews can be a win/win option by including the right questions.

An emotionally intelligent approach is characterized not only by a willingness to listen to all voices, independent of status, but also by a receptivity to the voice of the heart as well as the head. Sometimes the most innovative ideas cannot be articulated in grammatically correct, logically linear statements. Their origins may first find expression in terms of rough drawings or elusive feelings. By being open to such expressions of the heart, an emotionally intelligent organization can gain access to innovations at their early stages, even before a hired technical writer can figure out how to put it in proper English. This puts the organization a quantum step ahead of the competition.

An emotionally intelligent organization encourages the newcomers, the "outlaws" and the loners to be more outspoken through the sense of group cohesion and support fostered by being sensitive to one another's feelings, independent of hierarchical status. It takes courage to come up with new ideas, to buck the tide. The emotional support inherent in self-managed teams fosters such bravery.

THE "SNIPER" AND THE VISIONARY

One of the key elements of emotional intelligence is the motivation that comes with inner exploration and self-awareness. Combined with honest feedback and support from others, learning one's own strengths and weaknesses, and the ultimate realization of one's true potential in some particular area or niche are driving forces to success. When all members of a self-managed team are fortunate enough to share this growing experience, watch out—this is a group whose drive for success is to be reckoned with.

Enthusiasm grows most readily with ongoing support and honest appreciation, and that's precisely what an emotionally intelligent milieu offers. With enthusiasm and a focus on one's natural strengths, commitment to successful goals becomes relatively effortless. Instead of work, it becomes play, as Mihaly Csikszentmihaly (1990) has described so well.

While the rest of us may be enjoying this enthusiastic pursuit of success, what about the occasional individual who sets the rest of us straight by "sniping" at our successes? The sniper excels at shooting down our best-laid plans, especially when they've already been discussed and have achieved a level of consensus.

Somehow, the sniper has managed to avoid inclusion in the consensus-building process, for whatever personal reasons.

The emotionally intelligent response to the sniper is not to reject such attacks in a defensive mode but rather to focus clearly on the relevant aspects of the message. The sniper's bullet can be used as a final step in quality control.

It's often an idea from the fringe element that can make the difference between success and failure. As great as enthusiasm is in the drive for success, it can occasionally result in overlooking fine details that may become critical at some point. The sniper can supply the saving grace, whether or not it's intended in that spirit. By welcoming all relevant input, even annoying, negative input, the probability of success is enhanced.

At the other extreme from the sniper is the visionary, who may overlook the grimy details that stand between the innovative idea and its eventual success. This opposite fringe element is just as necessary to encourage the group to reach higher for success. Where the sniper comes from the grim reality of mistrusting anything new, the visionary has no reservations in accepting it wholeheartedly. Both elements are important in an emotionally intelligent approach to inspiring innovation that breaks new ground.

A number of years ago, the millionaire Eugene Lang was asked to address the students at his former junior high school. He was happy to do so and prepared to deliver the message, "If I can do it, so can you!"

But when he looked over the audience, he saw young people who were completely different from what he expected. He anticipated seeing the kind of students with whom he had gone to school, middle-class, white youths motivated to succeed despite the hardships of their European immigrant parents. Instead, he saw a hostile, cynical group more interested in drugs and gang violence than in succeeding at school.

In an instant, Lang switched his perspective. Making an emotionally intelligent decision to yield his own mindset in order to appreciate where his audience was coming from, he quickly realized what it would take to bridge the cultural gap between his expectations and theirs. Simply offering them the promise of success through hard work wouldn't work. They knew better. They'd seen the failure and despair of their parents despite attempts at working within the system.

Instead, he decided to put his money where his mouth was. He declared right then and there that he would finance the college education of any of those before him who would graduate from high school.

Suddenly, the students sat upright and took notice. No one had ever offered them such an opportunity. Four years later, all but two of the audience of 60 graduated high school, when only 1 in 5 were expected to. Lang made a difference in their lives, and they made an even greater impact on his. Lang had a rich and fulfilling relationship with each and every one of these appreciative students. This broke new ground, both academically and personally, because of an emotionally intelligent reaction to an initially hostile audience.

The visionary can look beyond grim reality and see possibilities that few others can see. Lang saw before him not a group of desperate hoodlums destined to lives of poverty and crime but rather a group with the potential to turn their lives around if they were offered a dream of their own—a college education. What Lang paid out in college tuitions he got back many times more in emotional fulfillment. Money may not buy happiness, but the emotionally intelligent use of it certainly created it, at least in this case.

CONCLUSION

The visionary can look beyond normal routine and see opportunities for change that the rest of us might miss. In the spirit of *kaizen*, the Japanese term for continuous improvement, the dreamer can look at possibilities for better products and urge the rest of us on.

The visionary can look at existing policies and point out what's not necessary. She can streamline procedures to get there faster by pointing out routines that have become outdated without anyone else noticing. Once pointed out, however, it becomes obvious to all, even the sniper. But if we've overlooked something in following the dreamer, the sniper will surely bring us back to reality.

The visionary takes risks. The sniper doesn't believe in taking chances. The visionary knows no fear. The sniper lives cautiously. The visionary sees through rose-colored glasses, the sniper, through a magnifying glass. The visionary is a "can-do" person, the sniper, a "worrywart." The visionary transcends, the sniper descends. Between the two is a spectrum ranging from wide-open creativity to hard-nosed skepticism. An emotionally intelligent organization benefits from both extremes and everything in between!

Different personalities bring to bear different qualities, each with its own benefits. In the next exciting chapter, we'll see just how such different personality types can best profit an emotionally intelligent organization. Find your own personality type and uncover your strongest potential!

13

Persuaders, Achievers, Listeners, and Fact-finders

O wad some power the giftie gie us
To see oursel's as ithers see us!

—BURNS, *To a Louse*

One of the most productive talents of the emotionally intelligent executive is the ability to perceive others' strengths and weaknesses so they can be most aptly matched with tasks for which they're most naturally suited.

There are many psychological tests available. Among the more popular in the recent past are those that divide personalities into four types:

- People-oriented *Persuaders,* who enjoy leadership
- Decisive *Achievers,* who enjoy meeting challenging problems head-on with self-discipline and stubborn determination

- Group-oriented, supportive *Listeners*, who are emotionally open and compassionate, and
- Detail-oriented *Fact-finders*, who pride themselves on objectivity and accuracy

The emotionally intelligent executive doesn't need to rely on time-consuming and expensive tests to determine the personality types of employees, though these may be useful to validate personal opinions. An understanding of only two human traits enables the correct choice of one of the four personality types for each employee: level of dominance and degree of expressiveness.

Those high on dominance and high on expressiveness are most likely to be the Persuaders. Those high on dominance and low on expressiveness are most likely to be the decisive Achievers. Those low on dominance and high on expressiveness are most likely to be the supportive, compassionate Listener types. Finally, those low on dominance and low on expressiveness are most likely to be the detail-oriented Fact-finders. These relationships are illustrated in Table 13-1.

Since expressiveness and dominance are such important indicators of personality type, it would be very helpful if you could determine, without much cost or time, a staff member's status in terms of these two traits. The good news is that you can. All it takes are six simple questions.

Table 13-1. Relationship of dominance and expressiveness to personality type

Personality Type	Dominance	Expressiveness
Persuader	High	High
Achiever	High	Low
Listener	Low	High
Fact-finder	Low	Low

To determine someone's dominance level, ask if that individual:

1. Tends to take charge or to be passively hesitant
2. Tends to be actively confronting or to be thoughtfully accepting
3. Tends to be intense and forceful, or quiet and retiring

If the answer to two or three of these choices lies in the first part of the comparison, then that individual is highly likely to be dominant.

To determine someone's level of expressiveness, ask if that individual:

4. Tends to be spontaneous, or more self-controlled
5. Tends to be impulsive, or more thoughtfully distant
6. Tends to be warmly outgoing, or more coolly reserved

Again, if the answers to two or three of those choices lie in the first part of the comparison, then that individual is highly likely to be expressive.

Now, by applying these six simple comparisons to any individual, you can easily determine that person's levels of dominance and expressiveness, at least as to whether each is high or low. You now have adequate information to determine, with a respectable degree of accuracy, into which of the four personality types that person most readily fits.

It's true that we don't live in a world where categories can be applied to people with foolproof certainty. But this process I've just shared is a reasonable, easy-to-apply indicator that helps to match employees with tasks on an emotionally intelligent basis. To use this approach to personality typing, it's best to understand the four personality types in more depth.

PEOPLE-ORIENTED PERSUADERS

First of all, Persuaders are great communicators. They tend to be upbeat and creative, self-confident and dynamic, warm and charismatic. They are great at sales and leadership. The most effective way to motivate them is through public recognition and the opportunity to share their achievements with others.

Emotionally intelligent Persuaders take responsibility for their decisions. They enjoy taking worthwhile risks, especially highly challenging ones, because they have the self-confidence that they'll succeed and thereby prove themselves worthy of others' admiration.

Persuaders are quick to decide and equally quick to act. One of our most persuasive presidents was the very ordinary-looking Harry Truman. He proved himself to the American public and to international leaders across the globe by making very tough decisions with timely efficiency. When General MacArthur questioned his military decisions in the Pacific Rim, Truman rose to the confrontation and ended up firing him. Truman was able to take the heat, and remains one of the most popular presidents in U.S. history.

John F. Kennedy was another persuasive leader who led us through some intense Cold War confrontations and initiated the quest to put the first man on the moon. Persuaders can move us with the fire of their passion. A single sentence by Kennedy, from his 1961 inaugural address—"Ask not what your country can do for you; ask what you can do for your country"—had the persuasive power to shift the American psyche to a higher level of national pride.

If I were to select a patron saint for each type, the one outstanding example of emotionally intelligent, persuasive leadership would be Archbishop Desmond Tutu, recipient of the Nobel Peace Prize in 1984. The son of a schoolteacher and a domestic in apartheid South Africa, and hospitalized for two years with severe tuberculosis at 14, this boy, through raw intelligence and a confident, dynamic personality, eventually rose to the eminent position of Archbishop of Cape Town, the most important slate in the Anglican Church of South Africa.

Tutu's impulsive, daring nature, characteristic of persuasive leaders, was dramatically demonstrated when the crowd for political reasons angrily attacked a black policeman at a funeral.

Tutu flung himself onto the body of the man who was now being stoned. Only when the crowd quieted down, did Tutu, now covered in blood, return to the podium where he was to speak. Like the true persuasive leader he was, Tutu demonstrated the spontaneous, inspiring courage so characteristic of this personality type. When confronted with challenge, they react decisively and, if necessary, aggressively.

Persuasive leaders have such a strong faith in their cause and their followers that they will go in directions others may consider extreme. Consequently, they win the trust of others and excel in their ability to encourage and inspire others.

DECISIVE ACHIEVERS

Achievers have efficiency and bottom-line results to offer in the workplace. They are determined, self-directed hard workers. They are great at heading short-term projects that are labor-intensive and are very resourceful at surviving under the worst of circumstances.

Achievers are capable of much devotion if they consider the cause sufficiently worthy. They are capable of extreme effort most other types would consider beyond the call of duty. True believers and defenders of the faith, Achievers are determined to get the job done and don't waste time asking why. Better to have the Achiever on your side than against you!

Achievers are doers, not talkers, and they act without procrastination. They'll persevere until the job is done.

A formidable example of an emotionally intelligent decisive Achiever, and my choice for patron saint of this type, is Meriwether Lewis of the Lewis and Clark expedition team that blazed the path for opening the American West.

Born in 1774 near the Blue Ridge Mountains where deer, black bears, wolves and beavers ran wild, Lewis was drawn to the challenge of the uncharted regions of the West. Even at the age of 8, he'd run off into the foreboding forest alone at night to hunt opossum and raccoon. President Thomas Jefferson's biography of him describes the itinerant Lewis as a fledgling Achiever: ". . . no season or circumstance could obstruct his purpose, plunging thro' the winter's snow and frozen streams in pursuit of his object" (Jackson, 1978, Vol. II, p. 586).

At the age of 15, he was described by his cousin as ". . . always remarkable for perseverance . . . great steadiness of purpose, self-possession, and undaunted courage" (Davis, 1939, pp. 360–361). At age 20, Lewis joined Washington's militia to quell the Whiskey Rebellion. A year later, after challenging a lieutenant to a duel following a heated political discussion, Lewis was transferred to the Chosen Rifle Company of elite riflemen—sharpshooters under the command of Captain William Clark. Thus he met the partner with whom he would blaze the path through the American West.

Starting out one fine August morning in 1803, Lewis explored the Missouri and Columbia rivers, made friends with the Blackfoot, Nez Percé, Sioux, and Shoshone Indians, and accurately recorded the animals, birds and plants unknown to naturalists at the time.

Determined and self-directed as are all hard-working Achievers, Lewis was the man chosen by Jefferson to explore the unknown West. Lewis overcame all the obstacles the wilderness threw his way. He had the intensity of desire to succeed against all odds and the physical energy to back it up. He chose his men with sagacity and was an excellent leader, considered fair-minded by all under his command. He was determined to complete his task of recording all the natural phenomena of interest he encountered.

Fighting torrents of rain and bouts of malaria, Lewis and his men persevered. Here is one of America's finest examples of an Achiever, fearless and heroic in pursuing America's early creed of Manifest Destiny.

Another formidable example of an emotionally intelligent, decisive Achiever, and a more contemporary example of this type, is Cesar Chavez, the first man ever to organize a successful union for farm workers in the United States. After his parents lost their 160-acre ranch in Yuma, Arizona because of their inability to pay back taxes, Chavez's parents and their five children found themselves homeless, and forced to live out of their old Studebaker.

Instead of going to school, Chavez spent his youth crawling under scratchy vines picking grapes, sweating in the hot fields and choking on chemical sprays. As an adult he volunteered to help with Community Services Organization (CSO) and was hired to help organize farm workers. But what Chavez wanted to do, in his decisive, results-oriented approach, was to form a true union for the poorly abused farm workers and this the CSO could not do. Though he now had the responsibilities of a wife and eight children, Chavez gave up his job, and became determined to accomplish what he believed in. With the help of family and friends and a commitment beyond the call of duty, he finally succeeded in forming the National Farm Workers Association on September 30, 1962. By the fall of the following year, through sheer commitment and determination, he managed to sign up nearly 1,000 farm worker families.

Many struggles followed, some of them violent. As an expression of his commitment, Chavez began a fast in February of 1968, and persisted until he almost died. "If you really want to do something, be willing to die for it," he said. What better example of devotion and determination!

By 1970, success was at hand and the United Farm Workers was born. But the struggle continued. In July 1988, Chavez began another fast, this one lasting 36 days. When a reporter accused him of being a fanatic, Chavez agreed: "Those are the only ones who get things done."

Wouldn't you like to have your share of decisive Achievers working on your side? None are more adept at the cardinal principle of emotional intelligence—managing their own emotions for the sake of organizational success. Yet there is that inner intensity, focusing on bottom-line results. They're fierce competitors in the marketplace, and their chances for success are fortified by their risk-taking, independent approach. There is no ambivalence—their way is the right way.

An even more contemporary example of a decisive Achiever is Hillary Rodham Clinton—self-confident, in charge, and results-oriented, so much so that she had to back off from her action-oriented involvement in White House activities early in the first Clinton administration. Or take the example of Bill Gates, head of Microsoft. Here's an emotionally intelligent Achiever who has created an empire through his risk-taking, competitive and pioneering approach to the software industry. That he took enough time off to get married and build his mansion in Seattle was another miracle, unless one considers that even his home is an experiment in software application.

At 40,000 square feet, costing about $40 million and under construction for over four years, Gates' new home is one of the biggest personal experiments ever, testing the limits of high-tech entertaining. As Gates told Walter Isaacson in an interview for *Time* magazine, "As you wander toward any room, your favorite pictures will appear along with the music you like or a TV show or movie you're watching. The system will learn from your choices, and it will remember the music or pictures from your previous visits so you can choose to have them again or have similar but new ones. We'll have to have hierarchy guidelines, for when more than one person goes to a room" (1997, pp. 49–50).

Achievers hardly ever play frivolously. They're too busy enjoying that next challenge just around the corner!

SUPPORTIVE LISTENERS

Supportive Listeners are great as close friends, of course. They're also great for company morale. They're reliable, dependable and loyal if treated decently, understanding and tactful. They consider others' needs before their own and are supportive and accommodating. Unlike Achievers, they're slow to make decisions and take action. They usually specialize in their skills and enjoy being part of the team with little need for public recognition.

Listeners live for social involvement. They just love people—
the more, the merrier. And people seem to love Listeners, for
they gravitate toward them. Because of this Listeners are great at
sales and public relations. They definitely are not the best prospects for the solitary activities of accounting or engineering.

Unlike his Achiever wife, or his Fact-finding vice president,
Al Gore, Bill Clinton is a Listener who loves to party. Remember
how folksy his first campaign was with the Clintons and the
Gores partying their way across the country? Once in office,
Clinton never stopped listening, with his chatty town meetings
and his "I feel your pain" support.

A somewhat ironic patron saint of supportive Listeners is His
Holiness the Dalai Lama—ironic because one would not expect
one of the most revered spiritual leaders to be a "best friend"
type, but that's exactly what he is.

"Dalai Lama" means "ocean of wisdom." The present Dalai
Lama was born in a remote region of Tibet's Amdo Province.
Each Dalai Lama is said to be the incarnation of the fourteenth
Dalai Lama of Tibet, and is chosen on the basis of divine oracles
and prophetic visions.

The current Dalai Lama was installed at the age of four. His
youth was spent in preparation for his calling by studying meta-
physics and the philosophy of religion. When Tibet was invaded
by the Chinese in 1949, the Dalai Lama became the head of the
Tibetan government but had to flee to India in 1959 when the
Chinese threatened to dispose of him. In 1989 he won the Nobel
Peace Prize.

Westerners meeting the Dalai Lama seem to be transformed.
They approach the visit looking serious and reserved, anticipating the gravity of meeting with His Holiness. But when they
leave, they're typically laughing, faces aglow, as they look back
to wave warmly at the beaming, friendly Dalai Lama, waving
back. His secret, if you want to call it that, is his attitude: "I feel
that the essence of spiritual practice is your attitude toward
others. When you have a pure, sincere motivation, then you have
the right attitude toward others based on kindness, compassion,

love and respect. Practice brings the clear realization of the oneness of all human beings and the importance of others benefiting by your actions."

When asked if there were people with whom he could really relax, the Dalai Lama replied, "My attitude is that if somebody is open and straightforward and very sincere, then very easily we can get this close feeling. If someone is very reserved, very formal, then it is difficult."

This quotation could be framed as the basis of emotionally intelligent communication. Relevance, sincerity and respect are the basis, and when you combine these with the open attitude the Dalai Lama proposes, you have a winning combination for successful and efficient relationships.

Although the supportive Listener does not need public recognition, sincere, private recognition is highly appreciated. Family-oriented and even-tempered, the supportive Listener can be counted on as an excellent team player who will do anything to transform conflict into harmony.

Listeners love to get into your mind and heart. In turn, they're happy to share their own deep feelings. Psychotherapists excel as private Listeners and talk show hosts excel as public Listeners. We tend to open up to Listeners because they really do care. Listeners provide emotionally intelligent meetings with the emotional fuel to keep barriers down and emotional openness high. Listeners have this power because they pay the price of authenticity. When others share their hurt feelings, the Listener hurts as well. It's as if Listeners live the role of High Priest of Feeling— their hearts truly ache when others hurt. In order to overcome such hurt, they yearn to get closer to others. And so they listen. And occasionally hurt. And then listen some more. They help keep the wheels of emotional communication turning.

Listeners are the ultimate "people" people. Unlike Persuaders, Listeners let others take the initiative, and accept supervision gracefully. They can be extremely loyal and, if their needs are met at work, they can work extremely hard. Of all the four types, Listeners appreciate the emotionally intelligent corporate culture the most, where much work is done in self-managed groups and where the hierarchy is fluid and flexible.

FACT-FINDERS

Fact-finders are the people most comfortable in a high-tech environment. They bury their heads in their computers and flail away happily at the keyboard. They're organized, methodical, emotionally reserved, yet friendly when they need to interact with others. What emotions are to Listeners and bottom-line results are to Achievers, facts and figures are to Fact-finders. They love numbers, charts, and anything that provides the precise information they need to solve factual problems, and create systems on paper.

Don't ask them to the party, however! To them, human interaction at best is a waste of time; at worst it's a frightening nightmare. However, in a crisis they can be depended on to keep their cool, while all about them may be losing it. Despite the fact that they don't have the leadership skills of the Persuaders or the quick decisiveness of the Achievers, Fact-finders are nonetheless essential, for they are the Lords of Information, an increasingly important function as we become more and more reliant on computer technology. Engineers, although typically lacking the charm of Persuaders or the warmth of Listeners, have always been an essential part of industrial achievement. "It is also clear," says British CEO Robert Hawley, "that business cannot function and therefore wealth creation cannot be achieved *without engineers!*" (1996, p. 224).

When the details of an impending crisis become too much for others to handle, that's when the Fact-finders shine. Fact-finders love details, especially when the pressure is on. Sherlock Holmes is at his best when a killer is on the loose. Robert McNamara was at his best during the height of the Vietnam conflict.

Fact-finders don't want public appreciation. Their reward is an analytical problem well solved at the height of a crisis. Public adoration is anathema to them. They'd rather be up to their elbows in details, thank you! Because they're not adept at social communication, they're apt to be misunderstood and typically unappreciated, but that doesn't seem to bother them. Unlike their Listener counterparts, they have little need for social acceptance.

I've mentioned two presidents—Harry Truman as an emotionally intelligent Persuader and Bill Clinton as a Listener. In the category of Fact-finder, Jimmy Carter comes to mind. Although he's now generally considered a great former president and probably the most active former president, he lost his chance for reelection precisely because he failed to connect sufficiently with his electorate, especially when the choice was between him and the affable Persuader, Ronald Reagan.

I'd nominate Wernher von Braun as the patron saint of Fact-finders, precisely because he was one of the few emotionally intelligent Fact-finders able to succeed in the areas of Listening, Persuasion and Controlling as well. A Fact-finder in the arena of rocketry at an early age, von Braun was eventually recruited by the Nazis in their war effort. At the height of the war, he found himself at the tightly fortified village of Peenemünde in northeastern Germany near Nordhausen, where he helped build the V2 rockets that rained death and destruction over London. Overcoming his typical immersion in details, von Braun rebelled against the violent nature of the V2s and was arrested and jailed by the Gestapo for lack of cooperation.

When the war was over, von Braun chose to work in the United States, eventually heading the NASA program and overseeing the Apollo XI project that sent Neil Armstrong to the moon. Von Braun was an excellent Fact-finder, attentive to details and keeping NASA well organized and functioning harmoniously, with superb quality control and a minimum of conflict. He was easygoing and thoughtful in his interactions with Congress as he kept government funds flowing consistently. He worked slowly and precisely to get the job done, and epitomizes, to my mind, the best of emotionally intelligent Fact-finders.

CONCLUSION

Whatever personality type you are, there's always the opportunity to balance yourself with traits of the other three types, if you should so choose, to make yourself a more well-rounded executive. In the next chapter, we'll look at how to acquire some of the traits of the other types. Once you've accomplished this yourself, you're in an excellent position to help foster such changes in your employees as well.

14

Emotional Surgery: Enhancing Your Type

He who knows others is learned;
He who knows himself is wise.

—LAO-TZU

Beyond maximizing profits, there are other challenging goals for the emotionally intelligent executive: first, to assign people to roles that best fit their personality type and, second, to help others grow to reach their maximum potential. As well, there is the challenge of creating self-managed teams that function well using the best combination of the four types for maximum effect.

For example, it's clear that a Persuader and a Fact-finder would make an excellent pairing, as would an Achiever and a Listener. Pairing opposites brings to play both sides of the proverbial coin. The ultimate matching would have elements of all four types for optimum balance.

But what if you're short of one or another of the four types? Do you do the best with what you have, or can you develop the missing links to balance what is lacking?

I'm happy to report that you can indeed develop the qualities of any of the four types, either in yourself or in others. In order to best understand the process of developing qualities that are not your natural inclinations, I recommend you start with yourself. I'll give some suggestions on ways to develop the traits of each personality type.

DEVELOPING YOUR PERSUADER SELF

Above all, Persuaders exude the confidence that they're clearly in charge, primarily through attitude and body language. Typically, they project a singular characteristic that broadcasts their sense of authority—stature, stance, focused gaze, tone of voice. Sometimes that quality is quite unique, as in Churchill's petulant cigar, Yul Brynner's shaved head, or Ross Perot's earthy metaphors.

Second, Persuaders are quick to decide and quick to act. Just as nature abhors a vacuum, Persuaders love to fill any gaps in leadership. A typical response to the question "Why do you want to be President?" is "Because the country needs my leadership!" as if no one else could do the job.

Third, Persuaders love to take charge, but they have the ability to make friends of those they command. They delegate with courtesy and respect, making others feel important and appreciated. They can do so in part because of their vision and sense of mission with which they're able to engage others.

Many executives tend to be Persuaders, of course, but occasionally executives may be of one of the other three types. If you're one of those, then this section is for you.

The first step in your Persuader program is to take a trip to your local library or bookstore to get a copy of Dale Carnegie's classic, *How to Win Friends and Influence People* (1936). That will be your working Bible for the next few months. An old classic, this book contains all the basics that will help you on your new path to developing your Persuader skills, to be added to the talents of your current type.

The next step is to engage in some self-exploration to get a sense of what really matters to you in the business world. What do you feel strongly about? What direction would give you a greater sense of fulfillment? This may be the time for you to take charge of your career and pull others along with you.

How would you enjoy spending most of your time at work? If you could choose, what changes would you make? How could you delegate more of what you don't enjoy, so you'll have more time for what you do enjoy?

Here are some more questions: Who are some of the persuasive leaders you admire? Think about how they look, talk, and interact with others. Which of those behaviors would you enjoy trying on for size? Who's your favorite president? Obtain a biography or video of him and immerse yourself in his character. Bill Clinton, who idolized John F. Kennedy, did precisely that to counterbalance his natural Listener traits with some persuasive skills. It made a significant difference in transforming Clinton's public image to that of a more stately president.

How do you react when you're under pressure? If you're a Fact-finder, you probably withdraw to your computer. If you're a Listener, you probably clam up. If you're an Achiever, you probably start overreacting by becoming more demanding. If you're going to develop your Persuader skills, however, you need to change your ways.

When the pressure starts mounting, Persuaders can deal with it by communicating even more powerfully, conveying their message with a greater sense of authentic sincerity. Having gotten in touch with your own sense of mission, you now have a base from which to speak about the direction you consider very important, and about why that direction might be important to others as well.

It's precisely your newly acquired ability to involve others in your own sense of mission that enables you to persuade them effectively. By connecting with others, you're now acting with emotional intelligence. Your message draws others like a magnet, as they become engaged in the mission. That's the magic of persuasion.

Persuaders are able to persevere in their determined way but typically with an engaging style. Rather than alienating the audience, they win their support. They do so by being open to the expectations and needs of their audience, whether that is a single individual or a national television audience.

On a more personal basis, whatever your natural type, to look more like a Persuader, you can be more mindful of your appearance, both in terms of dress and manner. As you develop your Persuader traits, you want to look more socially appealing, with fashionable attire and a "hail fellow, well met" demeanor.

When meeting someone for the first time, make sure to repeat the name, as you shake hands warmly, your left hand covering both clasped hands for a moment, as you offer a warm smile with direct eye contact. This adds to a sense of personal charisma. Whenever you deliver an address to a group, big or small, plan at least two aspects of what you'll say—the beginning and the end. Make the beginning direct and straightforward, starting in a clear, calm voice, engaging your audience right from the start. For the ending, make sure you have a concise, forceful statement that delivers a sense of your passion with a punch. You can let the middle take care of itself, or rehearse that too, depending on the significance of your talk.

To improve your persuasive speaking skills, you need only consider two other factors—rhythm and enthusiasm. For improved rhythm, take the time to watch how successful speakers draw in their audiences by periods of silence and by building to a crescendo as the talk progresses.

Once you get to the podium, plant your feet solidly, grasp the podium and wait. . . . All eyes are on you; your heart's pounding; a little bit of perspiration may be forming on your brow, but no one in the audience knows that—if your feet are well planted on the floor and you survey your audience in a slow, deliberate manner. Wait 5 seconds, maybe 15, as much as a minute if you've got a very large audience, and you're really ready to wow 'em.

Waiting builds the intensity, and therefore the power, of your message. Whenever you make a particularly strong point, pause for another few moments of silence to let your point sink in, or to let the applause die down if your talk is going particularly well.

I mentioned that you can start your talk in a natural, calm voice and end with a passionate punch. How you build from that calm beginning to the climactic ending can make all the difference in the world. Think of powerful musical arrangements, which begin with quiet, sensual passages and build inexorably through increasing passion to the eventual explosive finale. That's how Persuaders deliver their message. Starting with a bit of silent teasing, they begin speaking earnestly but in a matter-of-fact tone, slowly, almost imperceptibly, building the passion until the final punch line leaves the audience drunk with persuasion. Of course, for most people, it takes years to perfect these skills, so don't be hard on yourself.

If you're a natural Fact-finder or an Achiever, you may be wondering, "Where will I get all this passion to communicate to others?" The answer, my friend, will be found as you explore yourself to find your deeper sense of mission. For only if you are truly passionate within yourself can you communicate passion to your audience. Finding and communicating your passion is the essence of being a successful Persuader.

This may be a particularly confounding issue for all you dispassionate Fact-finders. You've spent all your life sidestepping the messy puddles of emotion so you can get the job done as efficiently as possible. If you want to cultivate some Persuader skills, you'll have to make some gargantuan, earth-moving changes in your self-concept and world view. It certainly won't be easy. You'll have to learn a whole new language—that of the emotions. And you'll have to leave the security of your keyboard and monitor. What awaits you, however, can be richly rewarding and fulfilling. And by combining the twin skills of Fact-finder and Persuader, you'll bring a rare combination to the workplace, putting you in great demand. You can become a leader among your Fact-finder peers, a Persuader with a gift for facts and figures, or both.

So how do you go about finding your inner passion, especially when you've spent most of your life avoiding it? There are a number of paths you can take: pay attention to your dreams; take a contemplative vacation, alone or with a loved one; read books on self-discovery; engage yourself in some form of self-discovery group; explore your roots in terms of ethnic ideology and/or the successful exploits of your forebears. Decide on one approach that appeals to you and carve out a space for it in your life. Otherwise, you'll lose yourself in the minute-to-minute demands of your busy life and you'll miss a lifetime opportunity.

DEVELOPING YOUR ACHIEVER SELF

Overcoming obstacles is the driving force of Achievers. Confidence, assertiveness, even aggressiveness when that's called for, make the successful Achiever.

In order to take on some of the qualities of an Achiever, your first step is to get into a program of physical fitness, if you aren't already. Achievers come from a place of intensity and typically treat the body as a source of immense energy. You laid-back Listeners and frail-bodied Fact-finders, hie thee down to thy local gym and get thee physical! You might even consider the martial arts—judo or karate—as your way to fitness.

For reading material, I recommend Wes Roberts' *Leadership Secrets of Attilla the Hun* (1985), and Lee Iacocca's autobiography (1984), in which he describes how he overcame being let go by Ford Motor Company. Iacocca got hired as head of Chrysler and then went about outselling Ford. His driving force certainly overcame that obstacle!

Above all else, an Achiever needs to be assertive. You accommodating Listeners and conflict-avoiding Fact-finders need to get busy learning assertiveness skills. The basics are very simple. An emotionally intelligent, assertive approach involves four steps:

1. First, manage your own emotions while you inform the other that you're clearly aware of his/her situation regarding the matter about which you're going to assert yourself: "John, I know you enjoy your weekends off, particularly this coming weekend in which you're planning to play in the golf tournament you've been looking forward to for the last few weeks."

2. Next, inform the other about your general situation regarding your request: "As you may know, the meeting with the Stonewall Company has been postponed till Monday morning so we could all digest the changes we've come up with and get the contracts modified. So they've got to be complete by next Monday morning—or earlier, actually, no later than Saturday at 3 P.M., so the changes can be ready to be signed by Monday morning. We're really in an extreme time bind."

3. Third, let the other know specifically what you'd like from her/him: "If you could put in a few hours on Saturday morning, enough to get these changes consolidated, that'd really be appreciated. You're the only one with enough knowledge about the deal to really consolidate it at this stage. You might be able to finish up by 11 or 12."

4. Express appreciation and any reward as a result of this extra effort, ending up with a confirmation of acceptance: "You should know how much your extra effort will be appreciated. In return for your sacrifice of part of your weekend, I'll make sure you have an extra Friday off when you want it and I'll keep this in mind when your evaluation comes up next month. Can we count on you for Saturday morning?"

It's hard to say "no" to an emotionally intelligent, assertive Achiever, wouldn't you agree? Achievers know what must be done and, if they can't do it themselves, they recruit others to join the effort. Even you accommodating Listeners and work-alone Fact-finders sometimes have passing feelings of wanting others' help. Here's your chance to fire up those assertive skills so natural to the goal-oriented Achievers who always seem to be marshaling forces around them. The phrase, "no rest for the weary" characterizes them well. So stop analyzing why things aren't working for you and get some help from others by becoming more assertive! Rather than trying to please everyone else, Listeners, allow yourself the luxury of asking for and getting a little help from your friends. Instead of letting all the others enjoy the glory of team leadership, Fact-finders, get your own group behind you with a little assertiveness.

Develop your inner strength by transforming any angry frustrations into emotionally intelligent assertiveness. If you're angry or frustrated about something, who is the most accurate target? Approach that individual with gentle but straightforward requests and feel the power of the Achiever. Here's where managing your emotions turns productive. As long as you remain honest and respectful, you can become a very effective Achiever. The fine balance between inner power and outer respect makes it work.

As you learn to be an emotionally intelligent Achiever, learn to maintain eye contact without flinching. And, if you're not already in the habit of doing so, learn to project your voice to communicate that inner power you're beginning to assert. Take a deep breath and speak from your diaphragm. Practice this in front of a mirror if it's new for you and become familiar with the feeling of strength that comes with it.

The biggest challenge in becoming more assertive for you Fact-finders will be to jump into action before you have all your facts analyzed. Whereas the Achiever is quickly decisive, the Fact-finder needs to amass all the facts and figures and then analyze them before coming up with a decision. In the area of investments, for example, the Achiever will decisively buy up the good deal while the Fact-finder analyzes all the numbers. By the time the Fact-finder comes up with the right decision, it's the wrong time—the Achiever has already grabbed up the investment.

Another suggestion for you Fact-finders: When the pressure mounts, instead of backing off and withdrawing to your computer as is your habit, learn to put the flame under your newly acquired assertive skills. Even if it feels as if you're redlining it into the aggressive area, that's okay once in a while. First of all, you're probably not coming across as aggressively as you feel (since it's so unfamiliar to you) and, second, it'll earn you some of the respect that Achievers enjoy.

As all other three types wade into this new, intense area of personal conviction and decisiveness, keep this advice in mind and you'll avoid getting into deep water: Stay true to your inner convictions. You'll get more done and, what's more, you'll earn more respect!

DEVELOPING YOUR LISTENING SELF

Did you ever wish you had more personality, that you could be the life of the party once in a while? Well, you're at the right page at the right time. In this section we'll look at how to get to your inner feelings and how to share them when that's appropriate.

For one thing, you may end up being a lot healthier. A great deal of emerging research illustrates the finding that those who have emotionally close relationships with others live longer and have fewer heart problems than emotional loners. Survivors of breast cancer with close emotional support, for example, outlived their lonely sisters by a significant amount of time (Spiegel, 1989).

For reading material that will get the coldest heart pumping with compassion, I recommend the short, little-known book about Ginny, *The Dog Who Rescues Cats*, by Philip Gonzalez and Leonore Fleischer (1995). If you're a cat lover, make sure you have a box of tissues handy. Of course, if you're a dyed-in-the-wool Achiever, you'll probably do all right with only a single tissue. For those who prefer people to animals, and haven't yet read it, get hold of a copy of *The Bridges of Madison County* by Robert James Waller (1992).

In the film *Mr. Holland's Opus*, Richard Dreyfuss plays a character who is immersed in the details of his music. He cares little for anything other than his music. He decides to take a teaching job so he can earn enough while still retaining sufficient time for his musical "Fact-finding" composing.

But over the years, he is transformed by his music students and slowly becomes a Listener, especially when confronted by his deaf son, who accuses him of not listening, even to sign language. At the end of his career, his students and now grown son create a surprise for him—an opportunity to conduct his now complete opus, with his favorite former students in the orchestra. People may respect a Fact-finder, but they love a Listener, especially if he hasn't totally given up his Fact-finding talents.

Why has Barbara Walters been so successful for so long in the incredibly competitive field of interviewing? Her trademark is to bring tears to the eyes of her interviewees. She brings out the Listener in most of her macho Hollywood types, no matter how impersonal they try to stay. Barbara becomes the ultimate Listener and draws her subjects into the fold, followed by her TV viewers. Everybody loves a Listener.

Listeners are irresistible not only because of their desire for intimacy but the willingness to share vulnerability as well. There's no getting around it—if you want others to like the inner you, then you've got to open up and sometimes be vulnerable. That certainly is not easy, especially for you Achievers and Fact-finders. It will be a stretch, no matter how you slice it. But you can learn to do it.

Start with someone to whom you feel very close and with whom you've built a trusting relationship, whether it be a family member or friend. Take some private, undistracted time with this individual and start by telling the most significant chapters of your life story. Get comfortable with the flow of your story, including the emotions that come with it. You'll probably cry some and laugh some, and you'll end up a little softer around the edges.

Then try this with another individual you feel close to, and adjust the degree of vulnerability to your level of comfort. Continue this process with more and more people. As you share with others, you'll find yourself listening more as well—it's inevitable. Pretty soon, you'll have the attributes of a likable Listener, in addition to your other predominant attributes.

As you enhance your Listener self, you'll be much better at emotionally intelligent management, better able to judge others using your feelings about them as well as your intellect. As I mentioned at the beginning of this book, adding emotional sensitivity to your logical judgment is like adding sonar to a ship: it enlarges your view and makes the voyage much safer.

Being a Listener does not mean being spineless and meek. On the contrary, it takes a great deal of inner strength. One of the best descriptions of this comes from Esther Hillesum, who was slaughtered by the Nazis at Auschwitz in 1943, but not before she wrote her diaries, published as *An Interrupted Life* four decades later. This brave, young woman in her early twenties voluntarily entered a concentration camp to help her fellow Jews. In her own words, "There are plenty of people who have a lot of 'heart,' but very little soul. A soul is forged out of fire and rock crystal—something rigorous, hard, but also gentle . . ." (1983, pp. 194–195).

DEVELOPING YOUR FACT-FINDER SELF

Someone's got to be taking care of the all-important details while the rest of us are busy Listening, Persuading and Achieving. Fact-finders are as essential as, if not more essential than, the other three types. If details are not your forte, yet you're in a situation where you've got to deal with details, at least some of the time, and you need some help in that area, then this section's for you.

As I write this, I'm serving as Administrative Vice President of a professional organization. As a mixed Listener/Achiever type working on my Persuader self, I was totally ignoring my Fact-finding quadrant. I handled most of my duties impeccably. But one particular project that involves much detail, the importance of which I underestimated, remains the victim of my procrastination. So let's learn together.

Most of us need to enhance our Fact-finder qualities. In fact, Fact-finder qualities can help to increase self-discipline. Many of us smoke, eat more than is good for us, and occasionally drink too much—even though we *know* better. So how can we become more self-disciplined by honing our Fact-finding potential?

I don't think reading material will be of much help here. Every time we smoke, we can read government warnings on the package; there are more diet books than you can shake the proverbial stick at, and magazine articles about diet as well; TV ads warn us against alcoholic binges. The information's there—that's not the problem. To paraphrase Pogo: "We've met the enemy and it is us!"

The first step is to acknowledge that part of being human is to experience feelings, desires and temptations. The next step is to engage your Fact-finder potential to create the witness process I described earlier in this book.

To do this, enter your Fact-finding mode and, eliminating all emotion, become intellectually aware of the nature and degree of the emotion you were just experiencing. Detach yourself from the emotion, become fully aware of it in a factual way and observe it from a distance. Say to yourself something like: "How interesting that the emotion I was feeling was..." and then describe it in as matter-of-fact a way as possible. By creating that distance, you gain a clear vision of, and a temporary mastery over, that emotion. If you can learn to do that, you can more easily control your urges to overindulge in unhealthy practices.

As an emotionally intelligent executive, you can use these Fact-finder traits of witnessing and distance to more easily manage your emotions. The management of emotions such as anger and anxiety is the most important principle of emotional intelligence, both in your role as executive as well as in your personal life. The jails are full of people who could not or would not manage their emotions of anger or greed.

A corporate executive cannot afford too many lapses in judgment. It's essential to be able to master an emotional urge at any given moment. These days, the media are unrelenting. An emotional spat between John F. Kennedy, Jr. and his girlfriend, prior to their marriage, was played over and over by the tabloid press. There's not much room for error. Tony Danza poked a paparazzo or two in the eye and his image was instantly tarnished. The Frank Gifford scandal is another example that comes to mind.

In addition to protecting your public image, managing your emotions can help you keep your cool in times of intense crisis. Can you imagine how the Apollo XIII flight would have fared if the astronauts had not had the presence of mind to deal with the details to convert their spacecraft into an emergency "lifeboat?" A degree or two off the narrow entry window and they might still be floating in space. Their lives were clearly at great peril, yet by staying in Fact-finding mode, they were able to manage despite the loss of most of the systems in their spacecraft. With the help of equally efficient Fact-finding ingenuity guiding them from Houston, the astronauts arrived safely back on earth.

A logical, dispassionate, clear-thinking mind has its advantages at crucial times when decisions must be made on the basis of insufficient and quickly changing information. A single, significant error in calculations on the part of the astronauts might have resulted in their being burned to a crisp as they hit the atmosphere, or alternately, bouncing off the outer atmosphere, helplessly drifting further and further from earth.

Seventeen years after the Apollo XIII incident, NASA had another major problem with a space vehicle, but this time, the Fact-finders were overridden by the Persuaders. As a result, seven brilliant and accomplished astronauts—including Christa McAuliffe, first teacher/astronaut—lost their lives. The Fact-finders—engineers and technicians—knew that the O-rings were unsafe at low temperatures, but the politically minded Persuaders felt pressured by the fact that President Reagan was to give a talk the following week in which he was to promote Star Wars and the space program, and by the arrangements made with schools across the nation to link up with the first teacher in space. As well, the space program was running behind schedule and NASA was competing with the European Space Agency's "Ariane" flexible booster rocket design. This was not a time to slow down.

The politically attuned Persuaders were willing to take the risk, ignoring the cautions spelled out by the more prudent Fact-finders. The Persuaders won the battle—but lost the war. The Challenger catastrophe set NASA back substantially, and ramifications of that critical decision still plague the agency, even ten years later. One effect, however, was a new respect by NASA (and many others) for the opinions of Fact-finders.

Getting in touch with your Fact-finder self means being able to arrange your emotions when necessary. The ultimate aim is to be able to make logical decisions free of emotional turmoil, even in times of chaos and crisis. But you need to practice this during normal periods. You can't wait for a crisis to do so.

To foster a Fact-finding mentality, take a period of time and focus on a particular problem that needs to be solved or a difficult decision that needs to be made. Put your attention on all the objective details you can think of, while ignoring any emotional considerations. Ignore others' possible reactions, unless their decisions on the matter will have significant impact. But avoid getting others' opinions if they're not directly involved.

Take time with all the objective facts and details you can come up with, especially those that can be accurately measured in terms of familiar units, such as time, distance, cost, and so on. Keep exploring and clarifying the issues in terms of these measurements. Stay objective in your conclusions.

For example, if you are thinking about purchasing a new car, some relevant Fact-finding questions might be about the make and model, involving distance traveled, finances, gas consumption and the less objective comfort and aesthetic factors. A more challenging problem would be how much to spend on your annual vacation, because this takes more subjective factors into consideration. But even these can be looked at objectively, by asking what leisure activities you enjoy the most and what scenery would be most attractive in terms of novelty or exotic quality. The challenge comes in objectifying human factors that are not easily measured. Researchers do this all the time and you can learn to do so as well.

A more challenging aspect of deciding on a vacation decision is in measuring others' reactions to the various options. It's hard enough to determine your own reactions, and much more difficult to predict those of others with whom you vacation. So a certain amount of guesswork is inevitable. The most helpful advice I can give you here is that the best predictor of human behavior is past performance. Look at how an individual acted in certain situations in the past and that's your best bet as to what to expect in the future.

PERSONALITY TYPES IN POLITICS

The most successful politicians are usually the Persuaders, followed closely by the Listeners, followed by the Achievers, with Fact-finders coming in last. During the 1996 Republican primaries, when it was down to Bob Dole, Pat Buchanan, and Steve Forbes, categorization into types was very easy. Dole, an Achiever, was challenged by Persuader Buchanan who might have won a personality contest were it not for his hard, right-wing edge. Forbes, a Fact-finder, had the money, but Fact-finders have a tremendous uphill battle against other types.

As the primaries heated up, Dole realized he had to overcome his Achiever image and flavor it strongly with more Persuader style. He revamped his staff and concentrated on change.

It worked. "I'm starting to loosen up a little," said Dole on a "Nightline" interview with Ted Koppel toward the end of the primaries. "It doesn't come easy to talk about who is Bob Dole," he concluded. But change is possible. The election became a contest between Dole, an Achiever/Persuader mix, and Clinton, a Listener/Persuader. But Dole's handlers mismanaged his public image, hiding his true warmth behind frustrating attempts to fine tune his persona in response to the polls, and Clinton had too much going for him to make this a real contest.

CONCLUSION

Whatever your personality type, you *can* change and develop other aspects of your personality. All it takes is determination, effort, and time. You've now got the necessary steps, recommended reading material, some well-known personalities to emulate and the support of this book. Now it's up to you. Once you've fine tuned your personality to your own liking, you're in much better shape to take an active role in leadership. With more self-confidence in your newly acquired social skills, your associates are more likely to look to you for direction and motivation. In the next chapter, you'll learn the stages of development of self-managed teams and how you as a leader can be at the forefront of that development.

15

Leading Self-Managed Teams

Among the Blackfoot tribe, whom I knew best, leadership was determined with good will and in a *synergistic* way: Tribal members accurately knew which individual was best suited for a certain task, and there was no enmity or bitterness about assuming such responsibilities.

—ABRAHAM MASLOW, *Future Visions*

In the past, overall direction in a business organization came from the top down; in the coming years, it will increasingly come directly from the customer base, in order to respond more quickly to the consumers' needs. This demands teamwork, and that teams become more and more self-managing. The customer has become the judge of excellence and quality. Team members have been forced to become more flexible, more adaptable to changing customer demands.

As a result, self-managed team members need to learn one another's jobs sufficiently to step into them when the need arises, so that the customer does not suffer because of staffing problems. The overall process must be sufficiently flexible to allow for the best possible final product. The focus is no longer on individual achievement, but on how to arrive at the highest level of quality, regardless of individual credit. Compartmentalization of tasks is no longer desirable. Each team member becomes integral to the entire process.

Although Abraham Maslow, author of *Eupsychian Management*, wrote the following in June of 1969, it was not published until recently. Obviously, he was very much ahead of his time: "I hadn't realized it fully before, but the whole of the democratic managerial approach—whether we call it *Theory Y management or enlightenment management*—can be seen from the viewpoint of essentially participatory, localized, decentralized democracy, with consequently excellent customer feedback and with control being exerted at the individual, personal, and grassroots level" (1996, p. 156).

FOLLOWSHIP—A NEW TYPE OF LEADERSHIP

Self-managed teams still need at least one form of leadership— that of facilitating communication among its members. Leadership in the conventional sense—taking charge and assuming the brunt of initiative—is no longer necessary. As a matter of fact, this type of leadership can be an impediment. Since the self-managed team functions with little hierarchy, all members are equally responsible for the final outcome. Leadership functions primarily to hold the components together.

It's difficult to find a name for this emerging type of team leadership. The term "facilitator" comes to mind, to facilitate or make easier that which is already taking place. Carl Rogers described this function as appreciation of the other's point of view. This is quite different from what we have come to expect from leaders up to this point.

The new type of leadership is actually more like "followship," in the sense that the best team leader is sensitive to group consensus so that the team members feel understood. The self-managed team leader neither leads nor directs in the conventional sense, but acts as a monitor of communication, to ensure that any breakdowns in the communication process are quickly repaired. She must be highly emotionally intelligent, an expert in conflict resolution and sufficiently secure to fade into the background until called upon.

Competition is not the motivating factor in this team culture. Instead, it is the challenge to perform in synchrony with others that inspires superior effort. The challenge to be one's best through common effort is a much more effective motivation than money or trophies.

A team spirit of excellence creates its own form of accountability. Money cannot be totally ignored as a motivator, of course. The best motivation is team esprit plus financial incentive. Each team member can be rewarded financially for the success of the team as a whole.

RESOLVING CONFLICT

If I've given the impression that self-managed teams have virtually no conflict among their members, let me correct that right now. When people work together in such a way that roles intermingle, overlap and even fuse occasionally, you can be assured that conflict will be ongoing. The key, however, is to make the conflict productive rather than destructive. It is the difference of opinion that is ongoing, but the opinions can give way to one another in a smooth transition from the less productive to the more productive. Occasionally, however, conflict can get out of hand, human nature being what it is, and at such times, the skill of conflict resolution comes in handy.

A short while ago, one of my clients found one of its teams in such a dilemma. In this particular team, Renee was the appointed leader; Philip, in charge of data processing, was an emerging natural leader; and John, in charge of production, was quite able in his job, but was feeling somewhat overwhelmed by

Philip's strident suggestions on how to "run the shop." Since John was dependent on Philip for data prior to making decisions affecting his own work, Philip began to take on a more demanding or bossy attitude as time went by.

Finally, John had had enough! He appreciated Philip's aggressive, go-getter attitude but resented more and more strongly his bossy manner. "I need respect along with his suggestions," he told Renee, the team leader, "not his lording it over me. His attitude is that I'm incompetent and that he has to tell me how to do my job. I feel resentful . . . His suggestions are fine . . . It's the attitude that bothers me . . . like a little dictator."

Since these individuals had had training in emotional intelligence, Renee asked John, "What do you think is driving this attitude? Where is Philip coming from?"

"It's a control thing," he answered quickly. "He's honed these tactics to keep his control . . ."

"Why?"

"Covering up insecurities."

So there was the answer. Now, John was less threatened and could approach Philip in a more productive manner. Having conferred with Renee to get her backing, he then had a talk with Philip. "Phil, I really appreciate your suggestions. Some of them are quite helpful. But I want to tell you that I need to feel a sense of respect for my own area of expertise. I've put a lot of thought into my systems and they work for me. At the same time I've benefited from some of your suggestions. But sometimes it feels as if you're trying to be my boss."

"I didn't realize that," Philip broke in. "I was just trying to make our team as productive as possible."

"I'd love to continue hearing your suggestions," said John in a reassuring voice. "But I need a certain amount of respect to come along with them."

"You've got it," replied Philip. "I'm glad you told me honestly how I was coming across. I guess I've been a little overbearing." A new respect between the two allowed the team to work much more effectively.

Such interactions are usually part of new team development. Highly competent individuals, eager to see success as quickly as possible, may occasionally step on one another's feet. Working out such areas of friction goes along with human nature and forges a stronger, more cohesive team effort for ongoing, long-term success.

The team leader acts as a sort of "immune system" for the group, apparently invisible when not needed, but acting in different capacities when necessary, according to the problem at hand. If two dominant personalities get into a struggle, the leader can act as a mediator. If there is a lapse in the communication process, the leader picks up the loose ends and strings them back together by ensuring that the noncommunicating parties "hear" and appreciate one another's perspectives.

It is of paramount importance that the leader is able to fade into the background yet be on call at any time. This doesn't necessarily mean that she will remain inactive except in crisis. On the contrary, just like the immune system that is constantly on silent guard, the emotionally intelligent team leader is always alert to the needs of all team members as well as to the overall process of communication.

FIRST GEAR: STARTING UP A SELF-MANAGED TEAM

How do self-managed teams begin? How do we make the transition from the conventional hierarchies of yesteryear? The following sections outline the steps.

1. Focus on Existing Problems

The first step is to acknowledge an existing problem that results in estimable financial loss—poor billing practices, sloppy marketing, unenthusiastic sales, poor morale, or communication breakdowns among department heads resulting in customer dissatisfaction.

2. Call a Meeting to Discuss the Problems

Next, call a meeting of all involved and discuss the problems candidly, giving all an opportunity to air their opinions. This process will probably start slowly but soon open into a tirade of frustration and criticism. This is good. The more intense the tirade, the more truth emerges, and the greater feeling of being listened to, then the greater the openness to change. If you anticipate a great deal of such expression, you might consider scheduling a one- or two-day retreat to allow for full concentration and resolution.

3. Introduce Self-Management and Allow Teams to Emerge

The next step is to introduce the concept of self-management and to allow the teams to emerge on the basis of perceived functions. This can be done at another subsequent meeting or on the second day of the two-day retreat. Naturally, an experienced outside consultant could be quite helpful for the retreat and, in many cases, indispensable, in order to ensure an objective view when opposing opinions arise. Depending on the personalities and the number of personnel involved, this corporate culture transformation might take weeks.

Have teams congregate according to particular functions and goals. These teams, ranging from four to twenty-five individuals, more typically from eight to twelve, have as their goal the solution of their individual and collective problems through cooperative team effort. This can be accomplished, with effective facilitation by an experienced consultant, in as brief a period as two hours or as much as an entire day-long meeting or retreat.

4. Give Teams Training in Emotional Intelligence

The next step is to immerse these individuals in some form of training in emotional intelligence, ideally a week-long seminar as described in Chapter 9. Preferably, those working together can be trained together. For obvious reasons, this will create excellent team identity and morale.

5. Cross-Train Team Members

The next step involves cross-training within each team to the extent that each team member understands the functions and activities of each teammate sufficiently to undertake those functions in that team member's absence. Although each individual remains indispensable, such cross-training allows for smoother flexibility and cooperation throughout the entire team. In addition, this results in a much greater appreciation of one another's efforts and enhancement of overall self-esteem.

6. Allow a "Settling In" Period

For the next couple of weeks, each team goes through the process of self-creation—beginning to understand in a comprehensive sense not only their teammates' functions but also their own working personalities. By the end of a few weeks, each team begins to take on an organic quality. Individuals become indispensable in a new way—not only because of the functions they serve but equally important, because of the integral support they provide to each other. When its members feel this organic quality, then that team is ready to work at full capacity.

7. Establish Communications with Upper Management

At this point, upper management can take the pulse of the change by setting up brief interviews with a sample of individuals from the various teams. This would also be a good time for department heads to meet with each staff member to discuss that individual's hopes for making a greater contribution to the organization and to explore forms of recognition most suitable for each.

A team leader formally appointed by management has the responsibility to report results back to management, but other leaders arise naturally from within the group. This lack of hierarchy allows natural leaders to emerge according to their inner sense of responsibility and manifest degree of initiative.

Formally appointed leaders meet among themselves on a fairly regular basis to ensure that the organic nature of co-operative productivity is not limited to the team level, but permeates up to higher levels of management. At such meetings, it is not at all rare for self-appointed leaders to emerge, whether because of scheduling difficulties or because of one or another's special interests or expertise. Both types of leaders subsequently share the information obtained at these meetings with their teammates and openly invite reactions and opinions.

8. Adjust for Optimal Productivity/Participate in "Refresher" Training

For the first six months or so following the introduction of self-managed teams, there may be a fair degree of shuffling among team members, until the size and membership makeup for optimal productivity is achieved. From this point on, team members can do new hiring themselves.

Subsequent emotional intelligence training sessions can take place once or twice a year from then on, for purposes of renewal and goal setting. These can be department-wide and involve the comprehensive reformulation of vision statements, first for each individual team and subsequently for the department as a whole. Since these statements come from the team members themselves, there will be a greater identification with departmental goals and therefore a greater degree of motivation to work toward them.

The groups are now off to a good start and function as self-managed teams. They are ready for the next stage.

SECOND GEAR

With so much ongoing, direct communication among team-mates, among their leaders, and between department heads and all others, there are fewer and fewer hidden sources of conflict. Those who were nonproductive but surviving solely because of their social skills are soon discovered for the dead weight they are, and are confronted with the choice of learning from their teammates how to become productive or else leave. Others may be revealed as having greater potential for new job functions and happily move into areas of greater job challenge, to shine even more brightly. Overall, for those doing the job for which they're best suited, morale is enhanced and bottom-line profits are increased.

By this time, the self-managed teams should be significantly more productive. The teams can respond more quickly to customer needs and with a greater sense of empowered respon-sibility than previously. Even product-development time is greatly cut because of enhanced communication.

The team leader, whether management-appointed or self-appointed, has the primary function of keeping everyone happy, that is, making sure members feel involved in the team effort with a sense of contribution, appreciation and personal growth through continuous learning and development. Although incon-spicuous as a leader, she remains sensitive to the needs and involvement levels of all teammates.

THIRD GEAR

As time goes by, each team becomes increasingly empowered, so long as support from management continues, to work with less externally imposed structure and more self-imposed discipline.

Administrative paperwork reports, wasteful and time-consuming, give way to streamlined decision-making. Customer feedback brings about quicker responses. Bottom-line quality is improved throughout. And each of the team members feels a meaningful part of the process.

OVERDRIVE

More and more, the teams become sensitized to marketing trends and shifting consumer demand. Response time is cut to months, or even weeks, instead of years. Each team can begin to make the decisions that pertain to its particular function on a nearly real-time basis, interacting on the basis of its interface with the marketplace.

Working more independently, front-line workers can acquire a greater sense of pride in their interaction with customers. They feel more accountable and put out a higher, more dependable quality of service. An empowered worker is clearly a superior performer.

Workers are now involved in the whole process, rather than performing an isolated slice of a function. This is much more natural human behavior. There is nothing more dehumanizing than being limited to a single, repetitive task, over and over. On the other hand, there is nothing more challenging than being a responsible part of a team process that goes from beginning to end. Sharing a large load with the team is far more meaningful than taking on a limited responsibility by oneself.

Although team leaders, for the most part, are not highly visible, they're available to make the final judgment on calls too close for others to make. They ensure that everyone on the team maintains the necessary level of training. If a team member does mess up, leaders ensure that that individual has the opportunity to learn from other team members. Ideally, this is done without the leader's involvement since team members can become quite sensitive to one another's needs. Weekly meetings can be a time for touching base with one another, and correcting any incipient problems.

CONCLUSION

Self-managed teams take on challenges as a collective group. The ultimate goal of meeting these challenges is customer satisfaction, not making the boss happy. Customer satisfaction is the criterion for success, not hours worked or tasks completed. The teams work smoothly because of emotional intelligence, shared among team members as well as between team members and their customers. Each team member is challenged to the fullest. There is no opportunity for boredom, or for empty glory seeking. Each customer transaction takes on a life of its own, and each team member is inextricably involved.

When things finally settle down, the new self-managed teams can result in:

1. A greater sense of meaningful individual involvement, resulting in high morale and company loyalty
2. More encouragement for creative potential
3. Streamlined productivity
4. Less time spent on meaningless and time-wasting paperwork and reports
5. More knowledgeable workers
6. Greater sensitivity and quicker response time to customer demands

Emotional intelligence is the lifeblood of self-managed teamwork. And self-management is the key to organizational success in the coming years.

With a more satisfying role at work, they will probably be happier at home as well. As a matter of fact, the skills of emotional intelligence work just as well at home as they do in the workplace, as you will see in the following chapter.

Part V
Beyond the Workplace

"What do you think creates a sense of enthusiasm? Where does it come from?"

"I'll tell you my opinion," answers Carl. "I think it ultimately arises from openness and a sense of appreciation. It also comes from working through the rough times, when things feel down and the going is toughest. Working through those low spots gives the group a sense of camaraderie."

"Accepting one another through the temporary failures," I add. "Seeing one another at their worst and still hanging together."

"Yes," continues Carl, "the honesty and authenticity that emerges from that experience brings the group closer together. It's ironic, but you can expect the most honesty and frankness when things are at their toughest."

"Yeah, like couples in the heat of argument. That's when the truth really comes out."

"There's little pretense then," explains Carl, "so both resolving the conflict of leadership initially and then dealing with the bad feelings when things get tough—those are the processes that help glue the group together. But it's important that the members trust one another enough to stick it through. Where that initial trust comes from, I don't really know."

16

An Emotionally Intelligent Lifestyle

'Tis but a base, ignoble mind
That mounts no higher than a bird can soar.

—SHAKESPEARE, *Henry V*

As the benefits in the workplace spill over into the rest of your life, it's worthwhile to explore the framework of a lifestyle enriched by emotional intelligence.

A FRIENDLY NETWORK

Loneliness kills—that's the conclusion of a couple of studies (Blazer, 1982; Reed et al., 1983) in which it was found that those who felt socially isolated were more prone to an early death. In a study of 7,000 individuals in Alameda County, California, Berkman (1979) found that, independent of other cardiac risk factors such as cholesterol and blood pressure readings, those who were socially isolated were two to three times more likely to die than those who had strong emotional ties with others. Having a strong network of emotional support is certainly an important health factor.

An emotionally intelligent approach to your social life would obviously involve fostering a number of good friendships to be maintained over the years. By being fair-minded and sensitive to others' feelings, people will be more drawn to you. To the extent that you can be emotionally sensitive to others during their times of need, they'll surely be more available to you at your time of need. Only if you foster such mutually supportive relationships over time will they be available to you at a level deep enough to provide the needed support.

Among these friends, you may be able to find one or two to whom you can divulge your deepest secrets. The complexity of life brings to bear difficult issues and only by baring your soul to these trusted friends can you best explore your own deeper values and work out the solutions that fit best with your character and integrity. Having such close friends with the opportunity for deep disclosure keeps your skills of emotional intelligence finely honed.

In this age of high-tech communication, there's less excuse for losing touch with a valuable relationship. If writing letters doesn't appeal to you and if phone calls are inconvenient, there's always faxing and e-mail. This way, if you meet someone you'd like to consider as one of your special friends, even if that individual lives far away, you can be in close touch through electronic media.

With the availability of such close friends and others in your emotionally supportive network, your problems can be dealt with, in real time, on an ongoing basis. Instead of letting unpleasant situations linger, you can take advantage of the opportunity to resolve them as soon as possible, freeing yourself up to enjoy the more positive aspects of your life. That way, you can reduce your worry time and have more fun time or productive time (or both together).

Making a habit of resolving problems as quickly as possible makes you more available to sense others' needs and to enjoy your time with others as well. You become a more attractive person to others. Being emotionally intelligent in a social sense means being aware of your own feelings so you can quickly detect problems as they begin to arise. Choosing sensitive and helpful friends is easier when you're emotionally sensitive. Being authentic means you can honestly disclose your concerns to such friends and be insightful enough to choose the best solution, maintaining a sense of integrity about the issues involved.

EMOTIONAL INTROSPECTION

Life itself unravels with its own deep wisdom. We can learn from all our life experiences, good and bad, by being receptive to what they have to offer. Just as we can be sensitive to others' feelings, we can also be sensitive to the deeper lessons of life's offerings. Even when unfortunate events befall us, there is something to learn, if we can be sufficiently sensitive.

By being aware of our emotions, we can evaluate the various components of our experiences and the decision points leading us to unhappy events. With such sensitivity, we can more quickly learn which choices to avoid.

This means taking a conscientious approach to analyzing what went wrong, at what point and how a different option could have been taken at various choice points. Going through some emotional introspection at each significant choice point can help us choose better in similar situations in the future. This mindful approach grows into wisdom as we mature.

LISTENING WITH EMOTIONAL INTELLIGENCE

Being sensitive to others' feelings makes it easier to communicate at a deeper level with family and friends. At certain times, however, it takes a concerted effort to break through the barriers of defensiveness or withdrawal when hurt feelings run deep.

Kevin, a financial wizard, recently appointed as leader of his team, was having trouble in his marriage. His wife, Karin, was at the point of legal separation. Kevin was dumbfounded—he had no idea it would ever come to this. Certainly, he had heard Karin complain over the past year or two, but he tended to ignore her complaints and go on with his own life. Kevin left it to Karin to take care of their baby and keep house, even though she had a challenging full-time job as well. Kevin felt it was her duty to take on both roles, while he "relaxed" his way through graduate school.

When Kevin shared his problem with me, I said, "Look, you've been ignoring her for over a year. Are you surprised that she's taken all she can?"

"I realize I've made a mistake," said Kevin, after some discussion. "How can I make up for lost time? I don't want to lose her."

So I taught Kevin about active listening. "Communication takes place at two levels," I told him, "on the surface—the words you hear—and the hidden emotions behind the words. Here's how you get to the deeper level, that is if you're interested."

"Sure, I am," exclaimed Kevin. "Karin means everything in the world to me."

So here's what I taught Kevin:

First, you have to be open to your own feelings so you can recognize them and acknowledge them. Only when you know your own feelings fairly well can you be open to the feelings of others.

When you're ready to really listen to someone else, you've got to be able to "empty your own vessel" to make room for the other's feelings. Repeat what she's saying, without intruding your own thoughts, until she's satisfied that you've really heard what she's said. To make sure, after you repeat what she said back to her, ask, "Is that right?" or "Did I hear you correctly?"

You may have to try to get it right more often than you think. People don't hear as clearly as they think they do. But when you do finally get it right, then see if you can identify the feeling behind her statement. You might say, "It feels as if you're angry (sad, happy, hurt) about it. Is that right?"

Now she'll have a chance to correct your reading if you're off-target. However, don't ever insist on your reading of her emotions. She's the expert on her own feelings; you just follow what she says. It might help to pretend you're inside her skin, as if you're speaking for her, but always with her direction.

It might feel strange to give up your own opinion and feelings while you're listening to her, but surrendering your judgment is only temporary. You'll have your turn after she feels completely heard. You won't lose yourself in the process, even though it might feel that way at first.

Kevin took all this in with interest. "Gosh, I've really been deaf till now. No wonder she's so angry at me!"

"It's not too late," I consoled him. "See if you can get her trust back. Let me know how it goes."

When I heard back from Kevin, things had improved some, but there were still miles to go. Karin was cautious, but at least she was open-minded. With conscientious effort on Kevin's part and the passage of time, their marriage will hopefully get back on track. If Kevin had had emotional intelligence skills at the outset, this never would have happened. Now, it might succeed in righting the wrongs of over a year.

CHOOSING FOR OTHERS AS WELL AS FOR YOURSELF

In addition to being open to the feelings of others, life is easier and more fulfilling if you can be open or receptive to what life has to offer you. Instead of rigidly expecting certain outcomes, you can look for the best in whatever is served to you. With emotional intelligence comes the ability to tolerate frustration more easily. If you don't like what's happening, you now have the skill to accept it calmly and see what it leads to or what you can learn from it.

Sometimes you come to a choice point and can't determine which of two paths to take. The emotionally intelligent choice, even though you can't determine which is better for you, is to choose the path that seems to be better for you and those close to you.

A short time ago, I was to give a reading from a novel I'd written. The reading was to take place in a large auditorium. Concerned that the small, select audience would feel dwarfed by the large auditorium, a smaller room was reserved as an alternative. The day before the reading, however, a decision had to be made because of the time restrictions in setting up video cameras and lighting. I wanted the more professional lighting available only in the auditorium, so that the video would have a more professional look. On the other hand, the audience would, in all likelihood, feel more comfortable in the smaller room.

Overlooking my own selfish concerns, I intuitively chose the smaller room. When the time for the reading finally came, it became quite apparent I'd made the right choice, even taking my selfish concerns into consideration. What happened was that a technician-in-training had been assigned to run the camera. When my reading finally began, Dorothy, the individual in charge of the evening saw a painful look on the technician's face. Without hesitation, she rushed up to the technician to realize that he couldn't find the button that would start the recording. A couple of frantic phone calls later, and the problem was resolved.

When I discovered this at the end of my reading, after a few moments of anger and disappointment, I realized that the whole problem could be resolved by recording the first ten minutes of the reading (the part originally missed) over again. This was simple enough to do. After editing, the end result might even be better.

Now, had I chosen the more selfish alternative to read in the larger, but darker auditorium, Dorothy would never have been able to see the look of desperation on the face of the shy technician. The whole reading would have transpired without being recorded. Moral? When faced with a dilemma, you may not know which choice is better. If the pull to either side is about the same, choose the one that benefits others as well as yourself. Chances are it'll come out better for you as well.

MASTERY OVER ANXIETY

Stressful incidents occur even to the most emotionally intelligent of us. No one is totally above the fray of life. We're all subject to that occasional unforeseen circumstance. So what's the most emotionally intelligent way to deal with such stressful circumstances?

When anxiety is the foremost emotion in response to such stress, the best approach is to create some distance from that feeling by labeling it as anxiety and then confronting the worst-case scenario. Labeling the anxiety allows you to view it from a slightly more objective perspective and allows the you/witness to feel some relief from the intensity of your anxiety.

Confronting the worst-case scenario removes much of the uncertainty from the situation and restores a sense of control over the situation. Having done this, the next step is to make a decision to obtain whatever expertise is appropriate. Illness requires a medical doctor. Threat of a legal suit or prosecution requires an attorney. Financial threat requires its own expertise. Marital discord requires a trained counselor.

Choose the best expertise available, consulting with those most knowledgeable in your personal network, and trust the expert's advice. Let the expert find the best solution for your concern.

Having done this, look at your situation as it might appear in the future—look ahead, beyond your present anxiety, to a future point in time when you can look back and visualize your present situation as if it had been resolved in a satisfactory manner. After all, is this not what usually happens? Most crises blow over and you can look back and at least smile with relief. By looking ahead to a probable resolution, you can gain some control over the impulse of anxiety, which, after all, is an emotion like any other.

And then watch your anxiety slowly slip away.

AN ENJOYABLE PROGRAM FOR FITNESS

Being sensitive to your own emotions means being sensitive to your body as well. We know our emotions through the beat of our heart, the pace of our breathing, the sweat on our brow, the tension at the back of the neck. With such sensitivity, you may find yourself more motivated to eat healthier foods and add some time to pursue physical fitness into your life.

As an emotionally intelligent individual, you can more easily defer the gratification of the couch-potato lifestyle and control the impulse to devour a fatty meal. Your sensitivity to your own emotions, and therefore body sensations, will give you ongoing feedback to maintain a healthy lifestyle.

Ultimately, you can enjoy the fitness activities you select to form an ongoing habit. To do so as quickly as possible, you can use the SPEAR method I've developed.

First, if you are a sedentary type, it is extremely important that you have a medical checkup as well as a fitness evaluation prior to starting your exercise regimen. Your doctor will most likely take a medical history, including questions about illness in your family, and perform a physical exam, including a blood analysis and an electrocardiogram. If you're over 40, an exercise treadmill study or stress test will pick up any apparent problems with your heart.

Now you can start the SPEAR program. Here's how it works:

- S—Set a goal: losing five pounds, fitting into your tight clothes, winning a trophy, running a marathon.
- P—Pick an exercise you like: one that is compatible with your schedule, fits in logistically with your life (near

a park, pool, airport, etc.) and, very importantly, that you also . . .

- E—Enjoy: not only should you enjoy the activity itself, but allow music, the right companion(s), sense of competition, or whatever to fulfill their roles. When running, I enjoy anticipating the Saturday morning road races. To each his own—find *your* own.
- A—Always do your exercise: make it a high priority in your daily schedule. Don't allow exceptions to become the rule. I discipline myself by not having my dinner until I've done my run or swim. No run, no eat. I usually end up running when I get hungry enough.
- R—Routine is extremely helpful: if I'm running, I make sure my running gear is handy and my walkman batteries are charged, so when the time comes, I won't have to be concerned with those things and become distracted. The same goes for swimming. Do I have my goggles and dry swimsuit handy when the time comes? If you can do your activity at the same time each day, all the better. The more routine the logistics, the easier you'll make it for yourself.

One factor outweighs all others in acquiring and maintaining a healthy body—a desire to participate in and enjoy disciplined physical activity that is challenging and satisfying. The key is to enjoy such activity and to experience a sense of fulfillment as one goes from level to level of challenge.

A fit and healthy body makes all challenges more approachable. With more vigor and energy, intellectual, administrative and creative efforts are more easily tackled. In addition, being fit contributes to a greater sense of self-esteem.

The key is to develop an appetite for such physical activity, if it isn't yet developed. Once fitness becomes part of your life, and you experience the stamina, energy and confidence as a result, you're a step ahead in terms of solving your personal problems.

USING SMARTER INTUITION

Just as being sensitive to your own emotions makes you more sensitive to body sensations, it can also make you more sensitive to that "gut feeling" or "sixth sense" we call intuition. By getting into the habit of emotional introspection, you can fine-tune your intuitive sense and use that to make even better decisions, especially when confronted with frustrating dilemmas.

Intuition and gut feelings are typically more reliable and trustworthy in the long run than what your intellect can tell you. Your brain works with all the data you're aware of. Your intuition includes all these data and then some, such as data at the feeling level that you can't yet articulate in thoughts or words.

You can't remember everything you see and hear, but all the information that enters your brain through your senses is virtually stored there until you die. You can only put into words or conceptualize a tiny fraction of all the data stored within your skull. The part that you can put into words is what psychologists refer to as conscious mind. All the rest—the data that can't be expressed in words because they haven't been processed by certain components of the "thinking" cerebral cortex—is called the unconscious.

When you make decisions based on your thoughts alone, you're using only a small fraction of your brain data. When you use your intuition to help you decide, you're using data that you can't put into words, yet you can still sense through your bodily feelings. Since more data are available with intuition, better or smarter judgments or decisions result.

In order to foster such intuition and inner wisdom, begin by taking some time each day to meditate in a comfortable setting, free from distraction. Try not to spend the time "thinking," attempting to solve problems. There are many books on techniques of meditation, but the goal is to tune in to that intuitive level of awareness beyond the conscious mind. In this way, you can begin to access those data that are not otherwise available and feed them into the decision-making process. You can then expect to make sounder decisions and wiser judgments.

CONCLUSION

An emotionally intelligent lifestyle ensures a longer, healthier life, through a friendly network of supportive friends, wiser decision making, more compassionate family relations, a generous disposition, mastery over stress, a fit body and access to your inner wisdom.

We can have a certain mastery over our own immediate world but the larger environment presents a much different challenge. As the workplace continues to suffer through this era of downsizing, we can take a different stance. In the next chapter we'll take a look at one potential—and creative—way to deal with downsizing and outsourcing.

17

Downsizing and Outsourcing

Commerce links all mankind in one common brotherhood of
mutual dependence and interests.

—PRESIDENT JAMES A. GARFIELD

It's one thing to talk about emotional sensitivity, quite another to
look cold reality in the face and see the newly disenfranchised in
the unemployment lines. The 1990s ushered in a new business
philosophy that had never been seen in the history of business—
laying off tens of thousands of employees to prune the work
force and watch the stock prices climb.

WHY DOWNSIZING?

Companies such as AT&T, IBM and General Motors have laid
off 40,000; 120,000; and 74,000 workers, respectively, between
1991 and 1996. Whether these cutbacks are the long-delayed
effect of automation, much discussed in the 1950s, or a
sacrifice of humans to the greedy gods of Mammon presiding

over an insecure Wall Street, they are a reality that cannot be denied.

Some argue that these layoffs are a survival mechanism to avoid raids from hostile takeovers, subsequently resulting in the same layoffs in an honest attempt at downsizing costs. Others argue that eliminating the last vestiges of protectionism by adapting to the legislated North American Free Trade Agreement (NAFTA) makes domestic labor inordinately expensive in the more competitive international marketplace.

It is clear by now that downsizing and outsourcing are more than a mere business fad. They appear to represent a new strategy in response to both long- and short-term economic problems.

INTERNATIONAL OUTSOURCING

As long ago as three or four decades, there were fears that automation and computers might result in the replacement of human labor. At that time, no one suspected that the real culprit would be an offshoot of the computer—the global Internet—which allows work to be downloaded from one country to another, totally bypassing international borders, customs agents and all the related paperwork.

"In the 19th century," claims Joseph Stiglitz, former chair of the President's Council of Economic Advisers and now a vice president at the World Bank, "the frontier of America was moving from agriculture to manufacturing. Today the frontier is going from manufacturing to services and technology, much of which can be exported" (Greenwald, 1997, p. 55).

American companies, for example, can and do outsource their computer work to engineers in India, cutting costs by at least 30 percent. Because of the difference in time zones, the work in India can be accomplished overnight as far as the Americans are concerned. The Americans e-mail their problems to India before leaving for home at the end of the workday and by the time they return the following morning, the solutions are awaiting them at their printers. This is great for the American companies, excellent for the Indian engineers, but less than gratifying for the American engineers who find themselves unemployed due to this international version of outsourcing.

An emotionally intelligent response to this challenge is to understand it as fully as possible and to adjust accordingly. Downsizing and outsourcing are two sides of the same coin. Corporate America has become more competitive than ever, as NAFTA and similar legislation have lowered the economic barriers between countries. American companies continue to compete with one another, but the rules have changed to include an international labor force, not only for entry levels in the manufacturing and production functions but also in the professional sector.

With such keen competition, companies are less able to afford the usual employee benefits such as health insurance, and retirement. Also, with an increasing resentment on the part of the labor force in general, strikes are an increasing likelihood, not to mention a greater disposition toward litigation in general. All things considered, a company is likely to feel more secure and more poised to compete successfully in the modern marketplace by outsourcing, rather than holding on to an increasingly unhappy and disloyal labor force.

JUST DO IT—OVERSEAS

Nike, for example, one of the most successful quick-growth companies, with an excellent reputation for quality merchandise and canny advertising, survives remarkably well without a single company of employees to manufacture its athletic wear. Without owning a single shoe factory, it sells well over $3 billion worth of shoes a year. How does it manage this? By hiring independent contractors overseas.

Like many other American companies adjusting to the new economy, Nike has become a purveyor of managed intelligence—eliminating its own work force and using its intellectual resources to hire independent contractors. The contractors are managed from a consumer vantage point (quality of the product is of the highest priority) or left to take on the challenge of excellence themselves. If Nike is unhappy with the product, it merely shifts to another independent contractor that can prove itself superior. The burden of competition is now transferred from Nike's shoulders onto those of its contractors. For Nike, this means no worries about employee benefits, strikes or, most important, fluctuations in the marketplace. Outsourcing allows for the greatest degree of flexibility, especially in terms of costs and quality. No wonder almost one worker in five has lost his job to the downsizing/outsourcing phenomenon in the past decade.

Even for companies that are not as lean and mean as Nike, computers help keep management apprised of how many and what kinds of employees are necessary for different projects. Whether the work is outsourced to local independent contractors or overseas, computers allow for an up-to-the-minute flexibility which is fast becoming the competitive norm. The result is less overhead, decreased liability and greater flexibility. Ten years ago, only about half of corporate America relied on outsourcing. Today, the figure is more like 90 percent.

THE DOWNSIDE OF DOWNSIZING

The benefits of downsizing to corporate America are obvious, but the unpleasant fact remains that over two and a half million people in the United States have lost their jobs due to downsizing in the past ten years. IBM itself, for example, has laid off over 120,000 employees. Yes, that's IBM—the former bastion of job security.

Much of the work force—especially those directly affected has become cynical, disenfranchised and embittered. Those who are untrained in other areas of work are especially vulnerable. Some, after giving the best decades of their lives to a single employer, have nowhere to turn when given the pink slip. It's a

208 *Beyond the Workplace*

sad tale, told over and over from city to city. The principle of company loyalty has gone by the wayside and has left a stench that is not easily removed. The untrained and uneducated are downsizing's most grievously affected victims. Corporate America cannot let this happen again. The answer is training and education.

We thought, decades ago, that the computer might be the problem. It would lead to increasing automation and eventual replacement of the human work force. To a large extent, it has. But now we've reached a turning point. Computer literacy is essential. It needs to become the first course of continuing education even for the most basic levels of the work force. It may well be just another corollary of "If you can't beat 'em, join 'em." Corporate America can no longer allow its basis of manufacturing and production to be victim to the downsizing phenomenon. If flexibility is an advantage to management, it can also be the same for labor.

THE INTERNET TO THE RESCUE

One of the benefits of computer literacy for the labor force is the opportunity of joining forces with one another on the Internet for purposes of reestablishing such lost benefits as group insurance and career outplacement. Insurance companies are happy to consider groups as customers, whatever the basis of their collective membership, as long as its members are not considered undue risks by the underwriters. As for career outplacement, the Internet is an excellent source of information on training and new jobs.

In addition, computer literacy offers the benefits of becoming employed as part of the outsourced labor force. Just as companies are outsourcing such functions as accounting and other clerical and secretarial jobs, the independent contractors offering these services need the people to supply their own work force. Computer literacy allows these individuals to join the telecommunication revolution.

The emotionally intelligent worker, even at the lower levels of the labor force, can look beyond the pain of victimization to see the opportunities that lie ahead in the new millennium—a flexibility that will never again allow corporations to have such devastating control over the destiny of the work force. The emotionally intelligent work force of the future will be much more self-sufficient and independent if it makes the computer a friend rather than a foe. The Internet can be a resource to organize for the purpose of group benefits, training, and insourcing—becoming a part of the work force by offering services to corporations on a collective basis.

INSOURCING—A CREATIVE SOLUTION

Insourcing is a direct response to outsourcing, and its natural consequence. Outsourcing results in the firing of current employees so that the job can be offered to an outside company that subcontracts the work. Insourcing, in which disenfranchised employees gather together to offer their common or complementary services on a collective basis, allows them to reenter the marketplace on their own terms, purchasing job benefits such as insurance and retirement provisions also on a collective basis. Just as unions are on the decline, such self-sufficient insourcing work groups may be their replacement.

What exact shape this new form of labor will take is difficult to predict. Just as the medical field has been tremendously affected by the growth of health management organizations (HMOs), totally unpredicted just a few decades ago, so may the disenfranchised labor force give birth to self-employment organizations or SEOs. Such SEOs could easily purchase their own insurance policies, tie in with HMOs for their medical needs, and provide credit unions and pensions for their members. The SEO of the future may be an emotionally intelligent version of what unions hoped to be in their heyday.

Even housing and education might become tied in to SEO benefits. Financial investment firms hired by SEOs could team up with their credit unions to offer attractive mortgages to members. Continuing education courses could be offered to SEO members to train them within the scope of its members' skills in order to enhance quality of service. Such courses could be taught onsite by its own members at nominal fees, making such education easily available to the SEO members.

Even as government downsizes its welfare benefits, the work force is further pushed to become more self-sufficient. This might mean that SEOs might organize among themselves to provide their collective members with safety net benefits that the government withdraws—medical benefits for the aged, mortgage protection insurance, and so on.

CONCLUSION

In the end, the vacuum in employee benefits created by downsizing and outsourcing can be filled by the disenfranchised employees themselves. The outsourcing revolution may give way to the insourcing revolution as something akin to what I call self-employment organizations arise to fill the gap. In a free-market economy, every need is seen ultimately as an opportunity for profit. Entrepreneurs can take the opportunity presented by downsizing and outsourcing and organize the unemployed into negotiable collective entities.

If new skills are needed in the marketplace, such SEOs can quickly retrain for the flexibility required in the new millennium. After all, that's what sparked downsizing and outsourcing to begin with—a dire need for greater flexibility. That greater flexibility may be arriving—with a vengeance!

In the final chapter, we'll take a broader look at outsourcing and downsizing, exploring how the information explosion is transforming the very fabric of the workplace, especially in the arena of personal interaction. A revolution is quietly taking place. Read on and join in!

18

The Future Workplace

To know that which before us lies in daily life is the prime
wisdom.

—MILTON, *Paradise Lost*

The structure of business is changing in very substantial ways. Outsourcing, in which more and more services are farmed out to companies that specialize in whichever services are required, is becoming more popular. This means that the concept of company loyalty is wearing thin.

As a result, the emotionally intelligent individual brings to the workplace a more independent attitude. There is loyalty to the group and to the project at hand and to the larger company to the extent that the loyalty is mutual. But survival these days means being quick on one's feet.

More than ever, self-knowledge and the ability to communicate effectively with many different types are essential if you're to be considered emotionally intelligent. As we put emotional intelligence to work and as we approach the next century, old, formerly reliable structures can no longer be counted on to provide the basis for values and direction. New paths are being

211

broken and those who lead the way will survive. This is not a setting for followers.

DEALING WITH THE INFORMATION EXPLOSION

The emotionally intelligent executive must know his or her staff in depth, not as components based on their traditional education, but rather as unique individuals with special strengths and weaknesses. The knowledge of these unique qualities and how they would best fit with particular tasks makes for effective executive decisions. The key concept is responsibility—both individual and collective—to get the right job done by the right people, with the right mix of talents.

The new executive intelligence requires the speed of an athlete to recover from sudden changes. As decision-making becomes more responsive to changing market conditions and less centralized, the ability to roll with the punches is required. Decisions are increasingly made on the basis of specialization rather than historical precedent. The more clearly the end result is specified, the clearer will be the path to its completion, and the more attainable the goal.

Because of the information explosion, where communication is more likely to be electronic than face-to-face, and where much more information can be brought to bear, decisions are made at each level of interaction, forcing higher-level executives to rely on the judgment of their staff. Tomorrow's "leader will manage successfully by consensus," maintains British CEO Robert Hawley, "rather than by compromise" (1996, p. 220).

In addition, the avalanche of information has forced the speed of the decision-making process. In the past, decision points could be measured in months, if not in years. Nowadays they're measured in weeks, if not days. Business occurs in a "stream" of events, in a very fluid environment. The emotionally intelligent worker is forward-looking, with self-knowledge as the key to career growth. This self-knowledge is based on current performance and the ability to learn quickly about new technologies, new markets and emerging demographics. Only the generalists who can interface with many experts will advance, leaving their uninformed colleagues behind.

MOBILITY REPLACES STABILITY

A decade or two ago, "international trade" was considered an exotic specialty. Today, we work in a world economy. Both money and information flow freely across borders. Increasingly, the American economy is wedded to the world economy, and this accelerates the decentralization in decision-making.

The emotionally intelligent executive in this free-flowing environment has to be a team developer, able to create harmony out of chaos when necessary, to persuade his/her staff members to work for mutual benefit in an environment characterized more by change than stability.

Emotionally intelligent team members need to be sufficiently adaptable in their specialties to move easily from one team to another, from one project to another. Such team mobility may be the key to success in the foreseeable future.

FEWER BUT MORE PRODUCTIVE MEETINGS

It will be interesting to discover, as we emerge from the current era of downsizing, whether the pruned work forces will be more efficient. I imagine they will. As sad as I am for those who were let go, I imagine that the smaller work forces will be operating at a higher level of efficiency. A more competitive workplace fosters a higher degree of executive intelligence as each individual's sphere of responsibility expands to meet his/her potential. A certain portion of people problems may be nothing more than territorial disputes over diminishing human resources and increased areas of responsibility. With a smaller work force, areas of responsibility increase and support may tend to replace petty bickering.

Take meetings, for example. With an engorged work force, meetings are abundant. If people have time for meetings, then meetings will take place—long meetings. With a reduced work force and increased areas of responsibility, meetings will of necessity be fewer and shorter. An emotionally intelligent meeting gets to the point, hears all relevant opinions quickly and allows for an emotionally open exchange of ideas until a group consensus can be felt, typically in a short period of time if emotional focus stays on relevance and sincerity, rather than on ego-driven struggles for dominance. The emotionally intelligent team leader acts as a facilitator of communication among others, not as a despot to be persuaded by others. This is the key to quick group consensus. The energy is focused on relevance rather than on dominance struggles.

HIGH-TECH MEETINGS

With high-tech communication requiring more interaction with machines, the workplace can become very emotionally sterile. This can lead to low morale, poor motivation and an increasing number of conflict hot-spots. Communication of feelings among those workers who do have face-to-face contact on a periodic basis can help overcome such problems.

Ultimately, whatever the work environment, bringing the heart to join the mind in the workplace enhances self-management through improved skill in listening, more effective conflict resolution and more efficient organization because of willing cooperation.

The current trend is not only away from "meeting-itis," but also toward telecommuting. Not only do people not attend meetings; they don't even come to work at the office. Telecommuting encourages people to do their work at home, communicating with the office through faxes and e-mail. This is especially practical in cities with daily traffic gridlock and with unusual or excess circumstances (such as Atlanta's hosting of the Olympics in 1996).

Telecommuting benefits both employees and employers. The benefits to employees who must otherwise commute through heavy traffic are obvious. The employers' benefits come from less overhead with reduced office space.

As team members begin to communicate in less hierarchical fashion, existing office structures sometimes become obsolete. Emerging over the horizon along with telecommuting is another new trend: an experimental approach to office design.

Often referred to as "cave and commons," this type of structure offers a flexible design in which team members can avail themselves of complete privacy in small cylindrical booths ("caves"), or they can use the adjacent "common" areas for casual, free-flowing meetings that allow for informal drop-ins or listening-in.

The caves can also be used as open cubicles surrounding the common area filled with information sources such as fax machines, computer screens, mobile file cabinets and other reading material. This allows for informal networks and more efficient communication of both common and esoteric information among team members.

This new emotionally intelligent office design is more compatible with the decrease in hierarchy in successful business settings. It supports the more informal yet efficient brainstorming approach where teamwork replaces the older linear model.

A center table made up of modular components can be separated or rearranged as needs change from hour to hour. Individuals can move smoothly from a large or small meeting to one of the surrounding cave cubicles, or "personal harbors," equipped with phones and computer setups as well as electronic whiteboards and CD players, to implement in privacy the decisions just made in the meeting held only a few seconds away (both in terms of time and space). If a team member suddenly forgets an important detail or needs access to a teammate's expertise, he merely needs to open the cubicle door and virtually tap that co-worker on the shoulder, or reconnect with an ongoing meeting for a brief interruption. Communication flow is remarkably enhanced.

Telecommuting, on the other hand, allows team members freedom of movement away from the office, while retaining many of the benefits of access to communication. Sometimes referred to as "work-anywhere-anytime" programs, it makes ample use of cellular phones, fax machines, voice mail, laptops and e-mail to communicate with both customers and co-workers from any place on earth, and even off it, as on airplanes.

A more recent concept, somewhere between telecommuting and the "cave and commons" idea is the concept of hoteling, in which private offices are entirely replaced by temporary spaces similar to the personal harbors mentioned above. In this case, however, the personal spaces are assigned and co-ordinated by a concierge much as tennis courts are reserved. Team members call in with their ID number and request a space for a particular time. Their requests are automatically processed within a minute, confirming their request or forcing another choice.

A staff member, acting as a concierge, accommodates fellow workers by overseeing the personal details of space assignment, such as having temporary name tags at the space and other personal effects such as hard-copy family photos to accompany those soft-copy photos automatically assigned as computer screen savers.

Mobile modules containing a desktop computer, phone and hard-copy files can also be used as a free-floating office to be used either in private or as a mobile accompaniment in conferences. Larger cubicles, known as bullpens, house from four to six people, irrespective of hierarchical status, on a more permanent basis, working on a common project. But even these are sufficiently flexible to be increased or decreased in size and/ or to be replaced by different teams entirely. Some companies, such as West Bend Mutual Insurance, have gone so far as to invest in a system called Personal Environment Manager, created by Johnson Controls Inc., that allows team members to adjust the air temperature to their liking as well as the portion of fresh air blown through incoming ducts. Independent research findings show a 3 percent increase in worker productivity, though some executives feel that figure is too conservative. They sense that productivity gains may be as high as 10 percent.

CONCLUSION

Whatever the arrangement, emotionally intelligent corporations are transforming their physical environment to foster a more flexible floor plan enabling staff members degrees of freedom they've never had before. Such changes in physical arrangement foster a greater sensitivity to emotionally driven communication. The breakdown in hierarchy, both in terms of office assignment as well as in status of function, allows for a more effective integration of information resources. Moreover, people feel more comfortable to integrate their personal schedules with work demands so there's a reduction in overall stress.

An emotionally intelligent lifestyle integrates personal with professional improvement. Parents of young children can use the freedom inherent in telecommuting to carve out the time to see a school play or final soccer game involving their child without any decrease in productivity. On the contrary, allowing personal aspects of family life to assume their rightful priority at special occasions inspires staff members to higher levels of motivation. Company loyalty, an otherwise diminishing resource these days, flourishes with such personal consideration.

In addition to using their time effectively, emotionally intelligent executives look beyond their own needs and desires to the welfare of those within the organization as well as those of the customers. The best executives focus their energies on supporting others. People live up to their expectations whenever they can, and a good executive sets these expectations at an appropriately high level within reach of the staff. Intuition and awareness of others' hopes and aspirations aid the emotionally intelli-gent executive in this process.

Workers no longer need to punch in at 9 A.M. and out at 5 P.M. like robotic automatons, resistant and hostile to management. The emotionally intelligent workplace inspires staff members to a sense of involvement and creative contribution. Freer to work at their own schedule, with a greater sense of trust and respon-sibility, they offer more creative and productive solutions to today's complex challenges in the workplace.

As we prepare to enter the new millennium, hierarchy is giv-ing way to flexibility, emphasis on status is giving way to a sense of achievement, and individual competition is giving way to teamwork. Executive intelligence has come to the modern work-place. The revolution has begun!

I've done my best to provide you with the most useful and practical information to help you implement emotional intelli-gence in your life, both at work and at home. But additional information keeps coming up as research continues on this most vital subject. In order to help you stay abreast of the latest news and information on this topic, I've initiated a quarterly informa-tion update, *Executive Intelligence*, to keep you at the cutting edge with the least effort on your part. A free sample of *Executive Intelligence* can be obtained by writing:

Dr. David Ryback
1534 N. Decatur Road, Suite 201
Atlanta, GA 30307

Appendix
Ryback Emotional Quotient Executive Survey (REQuES)

Assign a number to each statement as it applies to you, according to the following scale:

Always	Usually	Sometimes	Rarely	Never
5	4	3	2	1

___ 1. I prefer to keep others in line so that they do not overreach their assignments.
___ 2. I maintain a veneer of professional objectivity.
___ 3. I assign responsibility for failures to others.
___ 4. I avoid trying to influence or persuade others.
___ 5. I react to every problem with a show of anger.
___ 6. I avoid confronting discrepancies, trusting they'll disappear with time.
___ 7. I avoid emotional reaction to others' feelings.

Always	Usually	Sometimes	Rarely	Never
5	4	3	2	1

___ 8. I express my angry feelings.

___ 9. I keep my personal philosophy apart from my business personality.

__10. I display my feelings openly.

__11. I prefer generalizations to specific details.

__12. I maintain my focus on global issues, allowing others to take care of the details.

__13. I avoid problems, hoping time will cure them.

__14. I delegate high-priority problems.

__15. I make sure to keep my feelings separate from any public statements.

__16. I keep my "cards close to the vest."

__17. I listen to what others have to say.

__18. I focus on others' feelings.

__19. I judge others on the basis of their past performance.

__20. I take care not to be overly influenced by others' feelings.

__21. I desire to do good for others.

__22. Intellectual integrity interferes with my sense of authority.

__23. I am confident in my own abilities.

__24. I encourage others to greater levels of risk-taking.

__25. I am addicted to executive power.

__26. I am open with others about my own personal philosophy.

__27. Inner calm means more to me than spontaneous expressiveness.

__28. I enjoy my ability to influence and persuade others.

__29. Conflicts and problems are dealt with early.

__30. I have an open eye for discrepancies and attend to them early.

__31. I keep negative emotions at bay during any crisis.

__32. I am challenging without being abrasive.

__33. I offer support whenever I can, both in public and in private.

Always	Usually	Sometimes	Rarely	Never
5	4	3	2	1

__34. I express angry and forceful feeling in moderation.
__35. I am sensitive to personal boundaries.
__36. I make others feel as if they are unique contributors.
__37. I stay uninvolved and impersonal.
__38. I share my personal feelings and opinions.
__39. I am open and forthright in all situations.
__40. I allow others to lead without supervising them.
__41. I bring different factions together, even if they're opposed.
__42. I am open to opposing ideas.
__43. I focus on relevant details of problems.
__44. I take personal responsibility for unfavorable outcomes.
__45. I am candid with staff members about controversial findings.
__46. I make exceptions to policy to acquire important information.
__47. I delegate high-priority problems whenever I can.
__48. I am open to others' feelings, even in the heat of argument.
__49. I give priority to the feelings leading up to a conflict.
__50. I stay sensitive to the effect of expressing my own feelings.
__51. Spontaneous feelings are warmly and heartily expressed by me.
__52. I am able to obtain support and assistance easily.
__53. I communicate my intentions clearly.
__54. I am honest about my own feelings and intentions.
__55. I focus on others' feelings and intentions.
__56. I help others understand themselves.
__57. I encourage others to exceed job expectations.
__58. I enjoy complex challenges, and obtain satisfaction in sorting out the facts to clarify the solution.
__59. I enjoy complex challenges and find my work personally fulfilling.

__60. I'm just as aware of my human vulnerability as I am of my personal power.

ANSWER KEY TO REQuES

(Numbers in parentheses refer to corresponding sections in Chapter 10.)

1. *Never.* The high EQ exec doesn't keep others in line. Instead, she empowers (10) and encourages others to reach for the best they can be (1).

2. *Sometimes.* The high EQ exec fosters no deceit or preference and is emotionally forthright (3), yet is governed by a clear sense of propriety (6). This executive expresses enthusiasm and excitement through the ranks and, when called for, can show occasional feelings of anger (7). Yet all this is counterbalanced by an inner calm (9).

3. *Never.* This item is so obvious, it needs no explanation (4, 7, 10).

4. *Never.* This also needs no explanation (6, 7, and especially 9 and 10).

5. *Rarely.* The high EQ exec is frank, forthright (3), and candid (4), occasionally revealing feelings of anger and frustration (7).

6. *Never.* The high EQ exec is always open to resolving conflict (3) as soon as possible (4), to form clarity out of chaos (5), sometimes even expressing feelings of anger and frustration, but only when appropriate, and only in moderation (7).

7. *Sometimes.* Because of the high EQ exec's perceptiveness (2), expressive personality (6), and helpful attitude (10), she is certainly going to react to others' feelings, but maintains a durable, consistent center against undermining efforts such as gossip and manipulative favor-seeking (7).

8. *Rarely*. Occasional expression of forceful, angry feelings has a place in the personality of the high EQ exec (7).

9. *Rarely*. The high EQ exec is authentic and genuine, saying what is meant (3, 6), offering support through nonverbal means (7), and finds the leadership role personally meaningful (9).

10. *Usually*. The high EQ exec is authentic and free of pretense, expressing genuine, true feelings spontaneously, tempered with sensitivity as to effect (3).

11. *Rarely*. The high EQ exec often gets involved with relevant, specific details in order to clarify complex problems (5), as well as to resolve conflict (8).

12. *Rarely*. Dealing with specific details helps uncover the truth (5).

13. *Never*. Time, by itself, usually cures problems, but hardly ever in time to satisfy the high EQ exec, who acts quickly to resolve conflict (3), sometimes putting off regularly scheduled meetings when urgency requires it (4), taking initiative to confront discrepancies even before others become aware of them (8).

14. *Rarely*. The high EQ exec hardly ever delegates high-priority problems or procrastinates in dealing with them (4).

15. *Rarely*. See Item 9.

16. *Rarely*. The high EQ exec is authentic, frank and forthright (3), candid in the face of crisis (4), and pulses with vibrant personality (6). He encourages others through enthusiasm and zeal (7). However, when confronting discrepancies, he starts off with a gentle, warm approach (8).

17. *Always*. This is the essence of emotional intelligence.

18. *Always*. Same as Item 17, only more so.

19. *Sometimes*. Bringing out the best in others means accepting them on the basis of what they offer rather than what idle

gossip says. On the other hand, past performance, accurately documented, cannot be ignored.

20. *Always.* Sensitivity to others' feelings is crucial to the high EQ exec (see Items 17 and 19), but, when resolving conflict, she takes care to be open to both sides (4). She also avoids being overly influenced by manipulative favor-seeking or malicious gossip (7).

21. *Always.* The high EQ exec assists others in growing to understand themselves (2), and offers a model for open communication (6). He also is generally supportive through nonverbal means (7), aiming for mutual respect and propriety, even in the face of deceit and evasiveness (8). Candor in the face of crisis indicates trust and respect for the administration as a whole (4).

22. *Never.* Intellectual "integrity" does not prevent the high EQ exec from expressing angry feelings in moderation when that is called for (8). A vigorous, spirited personality allows for an effective sense of authority without sacrificing intellectual integrity (10).

23. *Always.* The high EQ exec enjoys the abilities to influence and persuade others, impressing others with the ability to make things happen, and feels competent in accomplishing most challenges (9). Above all she is confident and self-assured (10).

24. *Always.* By being warmly expressive and intensely involved in helping others, the high EQ exec encourages others to greater levels of risk-taking and achievement (10).

25. *Never.* The high EQ exec is not addicted to executive power, but finds deep fulfillment in personal relationships (9).

26. *Usually.* Openness about personal philosophy helps others know the direction of the high EQ exec and makes for better communication across the board (6).

27. *Always.* An inner calm helps the executive to be more sensitive to others' feelings (2). Although typically expressive,

warm and candid (6, 7, 8), the high EQ exec approaches areas of potential conflict with calmness (8), and counterbalances an outgoing personality with an inner calm (9). The "extroverted" personality has as its base an underlying inner self-assurance.

28. *Always.* An effective leader, the high EQ exec always enjoys the challenge of persuasion (9).

29. *Always.* Even before others become fully aware of them, the high EQ exec senses trouble spots—poor performance problems, conflict, low morale—and takes the initiative in resolving such problems (8).

30. *Always.* See Item 29.

31. *Always.* Although capable of demonstrating angry feelings when necessary as a last resort, the high EQ exec initially aims for mutual respect and propriety with a gentle, warm approach (8).

32. *Usually.* A receptive ear can calm those who are upset (4), and helps deliver clarity out of chaos (5). The high EQ exec invites parties of a conflict to paint their respective scenarios as early in the conflict as possible, and offers the benefit of doubt as much as possible, resorting to anger only when that is the only remaining alternative (8).

33. *Always.* The high EQ exec makes people feel special and unique through nonverbal as well as verbal means (7).

34. *Rarely.* See Item 32.

35. *Always.* In this time of sensitivity to issues of sexual harassment, there is no room for any lack of sensitivity to personal boundaries (7).

36. *Always.* See Item 33.

37. *Rarely.* The high EQ exec gets involved with others, making them feel special (1), identifying with their feelings (2), sharing his own feelings (3), and having an open ear to anyone

who can shed light on existing problems (4). He is enthusiastic and supportive (7) yet is quick to approach any area of possible conflict, being confronting when necessary (8, 9), and enjoys getting involved in helping others (10).

38. *Usually.* See Item 10.

39. *Usually.* See Item 10.

40. *Rarely.* High EQ execs stay close to staff members, encouraging them to greater self-understanding (2) and personal growth (1), dealing directly with problems that fall under their levels of responsibility (4).

41. *Always.* The high EQ exec brings differing factions together to focus directly on the challenges at hand, arriving at clarity in the face of chaos (8).

42. *Always.* The high EQ exec is always open to hearing both sides of any conflict (3), willing to make exceptions to policy (4) in special cases, and attends quickly to discrepancies, approaching them with warmth and sensitivity (8). She is open to all feelings from the gut (9).

43. *Always.* The high EQ exec gives priority to the facts leading up to a conflict (3, 4) and looks for relevant, specific details (5).

44. *Always.* The high EQ exec gets directly involved as problems arise and takes personal responsibility for unfavorable outcomes (4).

45. *Always.* As soon as possible, after coming up with a resolution to a problem, the high EQ exec makes new findings known to all staff members in as candid and honest a manner as possible (4).

46. *Rarely.* The high EQ exec is willing to make exceptions to policy in order to facilitate the discovery of important information that might contribute to the resolution of a problem (4).

47. *Rarely.* See Item 14.

48. *Usually.* See Item 17. This is where the rubber hits the road in managing with emotional intelligence. Even in the face of conflict, the high EQ exec gives priority to understanding the facts and feelings leading up to the conflict (3, 4). Uncovering deceit is accomplished by a gentle, perceptive approach, until there is no alternative except to fight intransigence with the vigor of an angry response (8).

49. *Always.* See Item 48.

50. *Always.* Although openly expressive, the high EQ exec is nonetheless sensitive to the effects of such openness, governed by a clear sense of propriety (6).

51. *Usually.* See Items 10, 38, and 39.

52. *Always.* By being very clear about intentions, the high EQ exec can obtain the support and assistance necessary to reach corporate goals (3).

53. *Always.* See Item 52.

54. *Always.* See Item 52.

55. *Always.* See Item 17.

56. *Usually.* With the wisdom of experience, the high EQ exec helps others to understand themselves, but not in a manner that comes across as pushy (2).

57. *Always.* By making others feel special and bringing out the best in them, the high EQ exec encourages others to exceed job expectations (1). This is enhanced by making thoughtful pairings between individuals and their challenges (5).

58. *Always.* With the ability to bring different factions together to focus directly on complex problems, the high EQ exec can probe the facts and emerge with elegant solutions, in large

part due to the ability to listen carefully and deeply to all voices (5).

59. *Always*. Dealing with conflicts quickly and courageously, the high EQ exec experiences work as personally fulfilling and satisfying (9).

60. *Always*. Keenly aware of the human condition, the high EQ exec counterbalances a sense of personal power with a sense of humility (9).

KEY

Score

To score the REQuES correctly, assign 5 to each correct response, 4 to any response that is one removed from the correct response, 3 to a response that is 2 removed, etc. For example, if the correct response is 3 and you chose 3, then assign yourself 5 points for that item; if the correct response is 3 and you chose 2, then assign yourself 4 points; if the correct response is 3 and you chose 1, then assign yourself 3 points. In other words, for each item, your score is the correct response minus the deviation from that number. Then add up all assigned scores.

240+   Superstar—you're in a position to be a great support to those around you.

180+   Star—with a bit of extra effort you can really get ahead.

120+   No prize yet—but at least you're honest. That's a great start.

60+   Nowhere to go but up—you've got a great future ahead of you if you apply yourself.

Bibliography

Adair, D. T. (1996). Personal communication.

Allen, F. (1994). *The Secret Formula*. New York: Harper Business.

Baron, R. A. (1990). Countering the effects of destructive criticism. *Journal of Applied Psychology* (75:3): 235–245.

Berkman, L. F., and Syme, S. L. (1979). Social networks, host resistance and mortality. *American Journal of Epidemiology* (109:2): 186–204.

Blanchard, K., and Waghorn, T. (1997). *Mission Possible*. New York: McGraw Hill.

Blazer, D. G. (1982). Social support and mortality in an elderly community population. *American Journal of Epidemiology.* (115:5): 684–694.

Boyett, J. H., and Boyett, J. T. (1996). *Beyond Workplace 2000*. New York: Plume/Penguin.

Brake, T., Walker, D. M., and Walker, T. (1995). *Doing Business Internationally*. New York: Irwin.

Branch, S. (1997). So much work, so little time. *Fortune* (Feb. 3): 115–117.

Bremner, B. (1997). Two Japans. *Business Week* (Jan. 27): 24–29.

Breslau, K. (1997). An enforcer with an edge. *Newsweek* (Jan. 27): 38.

Brisco, J. P. (1996). Competency-based approaches to selecting and developing executives: Current practices and suggestions for improvement. Executive Roundtable, Boston University.

Brooking, A. (1996). *Intellectual Capital*. Cambridge, Mass.: International Thompson Business Press.

Carnegie, D. (1936). *How to Win Friends and Influence People*. New York: Simon and Schuster.

Carter, J. (1982). *Keeping Faith.* New York: Bantam.

Carter, J. (1996). *Living Faith.* New York: Times Books.

Clover, R. D., Abel, T., Becker, L. A., Crawford, S., and Ramsey, C. N. (1989). Family functioning and stress as predictors of influenza B infection. *Journal of Family Practice* (28:5): 535–539.

Csikszentmihaly, M. (1990). *Flow: The Psychology of Optimal Experience.* New York: Harper and Row.

Daniels, R. C. (1996). Profit-related pay and continuous improvement. *Engineering Management Journal* (Oct.): 233–236.

Davis, R. B. (1939). *Francis Walker Gilmer: Life and Learning in Jefferson's Virginia.* Richmond, VA: Dietz Press.

Dayan, M. (1981). *Breakthrough.* New York: Knopf.

Dole, B. (1996). Interview on "Nightline," March 19.

Drucker, P. F. (1980). *Managing in Turbulent Times.* New York: Harper and Row.

Drucker, P. F. (1994). *Atlantic Monthly* (Nov.): 53–80.

Drucker, P. F. (1995). *Managing in a Time of Great Change.* New York: Dutton.

Dunung, S. P. (1995). *Doing Business in Asia.* New York: Lexington Books.

Evans, R. I. (1975). *Carl Rogers: The Man and His Ideas.* New York: Dutton.

Fenn, D. (1997). Rules of engagement. *Inc.* (Jan.): 49–53.

Gibbs, N., and Duffy, M. (1996). See you in November. *Time* (Mar. 18): 38.

Glasgall, W. (1997). The global economy. *Business Week* (Jan. 20): 14.

Goleman, D. (1995). *Emotional Intelligence.* New York: Bantam.

Gonzalez, P., and Fleischer, L. (1995). *The Dog Who Rescues Cats.* New York: HarperCollins.

Greenwald, J. (1997). Where the jobs are. *Time* (Jan. 20): 54–61.

Hawley, R. (1996). Leadership challenges in an engineering environment. *Engineering Management Journal* (Oct.): 217–231.

Hegg, G. (1971). 60,000 and counting. *The Economist* (Nov. 30): 71.

Herrnstein, R., and Murray, C. (1994). *The Bell Curve.* New York: Free Press.

Hillesum, E. (1983). *An Interrupted Life.* London: Jonathan Cape.

House, J. S., Landis, K. R., and Umberson, D. (1988). Social relationships and health. *Science* (July 29): 540–545.

Iacocca, L. (1984). *Iacocca: An Autobiography.* New York: Bantam.

Ikemi, A., and Kubota, S. (1996). Humanistic psychology in Japanese corporations. *Journal of Humanistic Psychology* (36:1): 104–121.

Ingram, Catherine. (1990). *In the Footsteps of Gandhi*. Berkeley, CA.: Parallax Press.

Isaacson, W. (1997). In search of the real Bill Gates. *Time* (Jan.13): 44–57.

Jackson, D. (1978). *Letters of the Lewis and Clark Expedition, with Related Documents: 1783–1854*, 2nd ed. Urbana, IL: University of Illinois Press.

Juran, J. M. (1995). *Managerial Breakthrough*. New York: McGraw-Hill.

Kelley, R., and Caplan, J. (1993). How Bell Labs creates star performers. *Harvard Business Review*, July–Aug. (71:4): 128–139.

Krackhardt, D., and Hanson, J. R. (1993). Informal networks: The company behind the chart. *Harvard Business Review* (July–Aug.): 104.

Larsen, R. (1987). Cognitive operations associated with individual differences in affect intensity. *Journal of Personality and Social Psychology* (53): 767–774.

Leaptrott, N. (1996). *Rules of the Game*. Cincinnati, OH: International Thomson Publishers.

Maccoby, M. (1976). The corporate climber has to find his heart. *Fortune*, Dec. (94:6): 98–108.

Malone, M. S. (1997). New metrics for a new age. *Forbes ASAP* (Apr. 7): 40–41.

Maslow, A. (1965). *Eupsychian Management*. Homewood, IL: Irwin-Dorsey.

Maslow, A. (1996). *Future Visions: The Unpublished Papers of Abraham Maslow*. E. Hoffman, ed. Thousand Oaks, CA: Russell Sage.

McEwen, B., and Stellar, E. (1993). Stress and the individual: Mechanisms leading to disease. *Archives of Internal Medicine* (153): 2093–2101.

McLuhan, M. (1989). *The Global Village*. New York: Oxford University Press.

Miles, R. H. (1997). *Corporate Comeback*. San Francisco, CA: Jossey-Bass.

Naisbitt, J. (1996). *Megatrends Asia*. New York: Simon and Schuster.

Norris, F. (1997). Will bad loans kill Japanese banks? *The New York Times* (Jan. 12): Section 3, p. 1.

Pennebaker, J. (1992). Putting stress into words: Health, linguistic and therapeutic implications. Paper presented at the annual meeting of the American Psychological Association, Washington, D.C.

Rabin, B. S., Cohen, S., Ganguli, R., Lysle, D. T., and Cunnick, J. E. (1989). Bidirectional interaction between the central nervous system and the immune system. *Critical Review in Immunology* (9:4): 279–312.

Rand, A. (1957). *Atlas Shrugged*. New York: Random House.

Rank, O. (1938). American Lectures of Otto Rank. In R. Kramer (ed.), *A*

Psychology of Difference, Princeton, NJ: Princeton University Press, 1996.

Reed, D., McGee, D., Yano, K., and Feinleib, M. (1983). Social networks and coronary heart disease among Japanese men in Hawaii. *American Journal of Epidemiology* (117): 384–396.

Ritus, R. A., Litwin, A. H., and Butler, L. (1995). *Managing in the Age of Change*. New York: Irwin.

Roberts, W. (1985). *Leadership Secrets of Attila the Hun*. New York: Warner Books.

Rogers, C. R. (1980). *A Way of Being*. Boston: Houghton Mifflin Co.

Rogers, C. R. (1995). What understanding and acceptance mean to me. *Journal of Humanistic Psychology* (35:4): 7–22.

Rogers, C. R., and Ryback, D. (1984). One alternative to nuclear planetary suicide. In R. F. Levant and J. M. Shlien (eds.), *Client-Centered Therapy and the Person-Centered Approach*. New York: Praeger.

Rosengren, A. (1993). Stressful life events, social support, and mortality in men born in 1933. *British Medical Journal* (Oct. 19): 1102–1105.

Roush, C. (1996). Coca-Cola's guiding light. *The Atlanta Journal-Constitution* (Nov. 24): H1–H3.

Roush, C. (1997). Coca-Cola shifts its state of mind on marketing. *The Atlanta Journal-Constitution* (May 18): E4.

Rovere, R. (1978). Affairs of state. *New Yorker* (Oct. 2): 135–141.

Ryback, D. (1996). (Unpublished ms.) *Beethoven's Passion*.

Salovey, P., and Mayer, J. D. (1990). Emotional intelligence. *Imagination, Cognition, and Personality* (9): 185–211.

Schmidt, D. D., Zyzanski, S., Ellner, J., Kumar, M. L., and Arno, J. (1985). Stress as a precipitating factor in subjects with recurrent herpes labialis. *Journal of Family Practice* (20:4): 359–366.

Shoda, Y., Mischel, W., and Peake, P. K. (1990). Predicting adolescent cognitive and self-regulatory competencies from preschool delay of gratification. *Developmental Psychology* (26:6): 978–986.

Smith, D. K. (1996). *Taking Charge of Change*. Reading, MA: Addison Wesley.

Spiegel, D., Bloom, J. R., Kraemer, H. C., and Gottheil, E. (1989). Effect of psychosocial treatment on survival of patients with metastatic breast cancer. *Lancet* (8668): ii.

Spitzer, Q., and Evans, R. (1997). *Heads You Win*. New York: Simon and Schuster.

Taylor, S., Collins, R. L., Skokan, L. A., and Aspinwal, L. G. (1989). Maintaining positive illusions in the face of negative information. *Journal of Clinical and Social Psychology* (8:2): 114–129.

Thorndike, E. L. (1905). *The Elements of Psychology.* New York: Seiler.

Thorndike, E. L. (1935). *The Psychology of Wants, Interests, and Attitudes.* New York: Appleton-Century-Crofts.

Waller, R. J. (1992). *The Bridges of Madison County.* New York: Warner Books.

White, R. P., Hodgson, P., and Crainer, S. (1996). *The Future of Leadership.* London: Pitman Publishing.

Williams, R. (1989). *The Trusting Heart.* New York: Times Books.

Yeaple, R. N. (1997). *The Success Principle.* New York: Macmillan/ Spectrum.

Young, J. (1997). The George S. Patton of software. *Forbes* (Jan. 27): 86–92.

Butterworth–Heinemann Business Books . . . for Transforming Business

5th Generation Management: Co-creating Through Virtual Enterprising, Dynamic Teaming, and Knowledge Networking, Revised Edition,
Charles M. Savage, 0-7506-9701-6

The Alchemy of Fear: Discovering the Power of Love at Work,
Kay Gilley, 0-7506-9909-4

Beyond Strategic Vision: Effective Corporate Action with Hoshin Planning,
Michael Cowley and Ellen Domb, 0-7506-9843-8

Beyond Time Management: Business with Purpose,
Robert A. Wright, 0-7506-9799-7

The Breakdown of Hierarchy: Communicating in the Evolving Workplace,
Eugene Marlow and Patricia O'Connor Wilson, 0-7056-9746-6

Business and the Feminine Principle: The Untapped Resource,
Carol R. Frenier, 0-7506-9829-2

Choosing the Future: The Power of Strategic Thinking,
Stuart Wells, 0-7506-9876-4

Cultivating Common Ground: Releasing the Power of Relationships at Work,
Daniel S. Hanson, 0-7506-9832-2

Flight of the Phoenix: Soaring to Success in the 21st Century,
John Whiteside and Sandra Egli, 0-7506-9798-9

Getting a Grip on Tomorrow: Your Guide to Survival and Success in the Changed World of Work,
Mike Johnson, 0-7506-9758-X

Innovation Strategy for the Knowledge Economy: The Ken Awakening,
Debra M. Amidon, 0-7506-9841-1

The Intelligence Advantage: Organizing for Complexity,
Michael D. McMaster, 0-7506-9792-X

The Knowledge Evolution: Expanding Organizational Intelligence,
Verna Allee, 0-7506-9842-X

What Is the Emperor Wearing? Truth-Telling in Business Relationships,
    Laurie Weiss, 0-7506-9872-1

Who We Could Be at Work, Revised Edition,
    Margaret A. Lulic, 0-7506-9739-3

To purchase any Butterworth–Heinemann title,
please visit your local bookstore or call 1-800-366-2665.

David Ryback, Ph.D. is a management consultant and speaker on personal and organizational success. His experience encompasses business management and government consulting, as well as teaching at Emory University's School of Business. His diverse client base includes the U.S. Department of Defense, government legal offices, financial institutions, manufacturers—both domestic and international, health care organizations, and national retail outlets. In *Putting Emotional Intelligence to Work*, Dr. Ryback brings many resources together to consolidate an approach to business that combines the practical with the thoughtful, emotional and intuitive. A new paradigm for leadership in the twenty-first century is clearly demonstrated.

If you are interested in having the author make a presentation to your organization, he can be contacted at (404) 377–3588 or:
David Ryback and Associates
1534 N. Decatur Road, Suite 201
Atlanta, GA 30307

THE KNOWLEDGE EVOLUTION
Expanding Organizational Intelligence
by Verna Allee

The Knowledge Evolution offers a unique and powerful road map for understanding knowledge creation, learning, and performance in everyday work.

"A must read for all organizational leaders who want to bring order to the chaos."
-**Jay C. Wilber**, General Motors Corporation

1997 / 0-7506-9842-X

. . . .

BEYOND STRATEGIC VISION
Effective Corporate Action with Hoshin Planning
by Michael Cowley and Ellen Domb

"Success in a highly competitive world requires focus and direction. This book will benefit any organization. It provides a template for process-driven thinking which will create bottom-line results."

-**Stuart Levine**, CEO, Stuart Levine & Associates
LLC, coauthor, *The Leader in You*

1997 / 0-7506-9843-8

. . . .

THE TRANSFORMATION OF MANAGEMENT
by Mike Davidson

Packed with compelling insights and vivid illustrations, *The Transformation of Management* is a comprehensive guide to the way organizations will need to be managed if they are to survive and succeed in the new global economy.

"This book is a genuine 'must-read' by senior business management."
-**Philip Kotler**, Northwestern University

1996 / 0-7506-9814-4

. . . .

DRUCKER ON ASIA
The Drucker - Nakauchi Dialogue
by Peter F. Drucker and Isao Nakauchi

Drucker on Asia is the result of extensive dialogue between two of the world's leading business figures, Peter Drucker and Isao Nakauchi. Their dialogue considers the changes occuring in the economic world today and identifies the challenges that free markets and free enterprises now face with specific reference to China and Japan.

1997 / 0-7506-3132-5

. . . .

BUSINESS AND THE FEMININE PRINCIPLE
The Untapped Resource
by Carol R. Frenier

"This very personal and quietly passionate book asks us to explore aspects of human nature that have gone unregarded for too long."

-**Margaret Wheatley**, author, *Leadership and the New Science* and *A Simpler Way*

1997 / 0-7506-9829-2

. . . .

POWER PARTNERING
A Strategy for Business Excellence in the 21st Century
by Sean Gadman

Power Partnering is a brilliant yet refreshingly simple approach that breaks innovative thinking and acting down into four distinct contexts, allowing people to respond to complex situations in highly creative and innovative ways.

1997 / 0-7506-9809-8

. . . .

CULTIVATING COMMON GROUND
Releasing the Power of Relationships at Work
by Daniel S. Hanson

"This is a compassionate and powerful call for caring in the workplace. Dan Hanson is right on the mark when he suggests that we need to take courageous steps toward a new, caring workplace."

-**Richard J. Leider**, founding partner, The Venture Group, author, *Repacking Your Bags* and *The Power of Purpose*

1997 / 0-7506-9832-2

. . . .

THE BREAKDOWN OF HIERARCHY
Communicating in the Evolving Workplace
by Eugene Marlow and Patricia O'Connor Wilson

"If you've ever doubted the vital role of effective communications in today's rapidly changing organizations, read this book. It makes a compelling case not only for linking communications to strategy, but also for making effective communication an essential part of everyone's responsibility-from the CEO to the newest hire."

-**John Alexander**, VP, Communications, Center for Creative Leadership

1997 / 0-7506-9746-6

. . . .

AESOP'S MANAGEMENT FABLES
by Dick McCann and Jan Stewart

This lively and imaginative book illustrates and suggests solutions for common management problems using the age-old device of story-telling. It is a fascinating book to help managers understand the people they work with, and for management trainers who want their message to stick!

1997 / 0-7506-3341-7

. . . .

LEARNING TO READ THE SIGNS
Reclaiming Pragmatism in Business
by F. Byron Nahser

"I will be surprised if this book does not altogether change the way Americans of the 21st century understand the place of business in American culture."

-**Kenneth L. Woodward**, *Newsweek*

1997 / 0-7506-9901-9

. . . .

5th GENERATION MANAGEMENT
Co-creating Through Virtual Enterprising, Dynamic Teaming, and Knowledge Networking, Revised Edition
by Charles M. Savage

"In 1991 I named *Fifth Generation Management* my business book of the year. I find the new subtitle of this revised edition *Co-creating Through Virtual Enterprising, Dynamic Teaming, and Knowledge Networking*, captures exceptionally well the shift in focus over the last five years..."

-**Tom Peters**, *from the Foreword*

1996 / 0-7506-9701-6

. . . .

LEADERSHIP IN A CHALLENGING WORLD
A Sacred Journey
by Barbara Shipka

"...a new and comprehensive guide to the really challenging issues and personal responsibilites of leading an organization."

-**Hazel Henderson**, author, *Paradigms in Progress* and *Building a Win-Win World*

1996 / 0-7506-9750-4

. . . .

SUN TZU ON MANAGEMENT
The Art of War in Contemporary
Business Strategy
by Foo Check Teck

A unique approach to Strategic Management; relating metaphorically relevant segments of the 2,500 year old classic Sun Tzu's *Art of War* to insights gained through analyses of strategy processes within major ASEAN corporations.

1996 / 981-00-6799-2

. . . .

FLIGHT OF THE PHOENIX
Soaring to Success in the 21st Century
by John Whiteside and Sandra Egli

Flight of the Phoenix provides insights to the series of management initiatives sweeping the workplace, such as reengineering, restructuring, and reinvention.

1996 / 0-7506-9798-9

. . . .

BEYOND TIME MANAGEMENT
Business with Purpose
by Robert A. Wright

"The power of purpose is presented with undeniable directness and simplicity. It helped me understand the concept much more deeply and presented a most significant inspiration and challenge."

-**Michael Allen**, President, Zwell International

1997 / 0-7506-9799-7

. . . .

These books are available from all good bookstores
or in case of difficulty call: 1-800-366-2665 in the US or
+44-1865-310366 in Europe and the UK

. . . .

An e-mail mailing list giving information on latest releases, special promotions/offers and other news relating to Butterworth-Heinemann business titles is available. To subscribe, send an e-mail message to majordomo@world.std.com. Include in message body (not in subject line) subscribe bh-business

. . . .

Feel free to visit our web site at: http://www.bh.com